AI vs CYBERSECURITY

Navigating the Battlefield of the

Future

Krishna Chaganti (CEH,CISM)

Contents

INTRODUCTION

AI in cybersecurity is like two sides of a coin. One side is where threat actors are taking advantage of AI advancements to infiltrate systems and networks and steal confidential information. The other side is where the white hat guys, or the good guys, work assiduously by leveraging artificial intelligence to protect endpoints and secure systems and networks. While generative AI and automation have been productive in threat cybersecurity, hackers are also finding great use in AI to perform their nefarious activities.

Mitrovic, a tech blogger, recently posted about his experience with a new tactic developed by scammers targeting Gmail users. According to him, they can request that you recover your mail. As soon as you grant that request, the threat actor will wipe all your data secretly. This is how it works, according to him. You will receive a notification or email with urgent instructions to recover your mail. Despite not initiating any recovery request, you will still get this message, which usually comes from another country. Let's say you decline; you will be called by an official Google number (which is fake). Once you fall for the trap that the call is genuine, the scammer informs you your account has been logged in from another country and then creates an urgency for you to approve the request to recover. The scammers then access your account and can proceed to use your data for fraudulent activities.

Another method is getting called by a fake Google number, where scammers use an audio deepfake coupled with AI-generated mail that appears more real. Before now, you could detect phishing emails by typos and inconsistent brand assets on the email. Right now, GenAI is creating a perfect email with convincing pictures.

The recent deepfake scam, which targeted a Chinese company and cost the company 26 million euros, is a notable example of how malicious AI can be deployed. There is no doubt AI is gaining traction across industries and sectors, but this revolution and fast adoption also come with concerns.

Here are a few of several cyber threats and trends that are worrisome and should be a major concern for individuals, corporations, and the government.

The proliferation of deepfakes

Researchers have described deepfake as one of the most dangerous cases of AI use. In light of recent elections and several instances recorded on how scammers have used deepfakes to trick corporate leaders, the time to understand how it works is now so you can stay ahead of threat actors. A study conducted by Onfido revealed that fraud attempts that used deepfakes surged by 3000% over the past year. This trend has been forecasted to continue, especially in the area of financial scams. Have you realized robbers don't enter banks like before? The theft of the future is cyber and AI-enhanced. The lock and key won't save any vault; it is time to be proactive. While deepfakes are becoming more convincing as AI learns and gets better, the imminent threat is also becoming large-scale.

Deep scams

This technique does not necessarily require manipulating audiovisuals. With the help of automation, cybercriminals can target a large number of victims. Imagine sending an automated email to a thousand Gmail users compared to 5 or 10 users before the advent of AI. For every scam that can be implemented manually, there is now an automated adaptation covering different malicious activities. This is also a concern as AI meets cybersecurity.

Large Language Models-Enabled Malware.

Researchers have uncovered three worms that can rewrite and replicate their code. By using the API of OpenAI, worms can use GPT to produce unique code for specific targets to be infected. While OpenAI has a blacklist of malicious activities, threat actors can download the LLM to a personal server, rendering blacklisting technique inconsequential.

Security researchers at the University of California, San Diego, and Nanyang Technological University, Singapore, have uncovered how an LLM can collate personally identifiable information (PII), including names, payment card details, ID numbers, mailing addresses, and email addresses shared with chatbots, and share the details with hackers. Privacy concerns around AI chatbots are also something to worry about.

Enough said about the threat actor side; let's talk about the defender's side. The truth is AI is here to stay. We see how large language models are helping security teams sift through a vast amount of data to produce credible insights through simple queries.

Despite all of this progress, there are still limitations in appreciating the details of specialized datasets in cybersecurity. The more reason researchers are now transitioning into more agile and specialized models to produce required insights.

My aim in writing this book is to answer the question," What are the challenges of cybersecurity with AI?"

How does AI affect different domains of cybersecurity, and what are the ways to stay proactive and resilient against AI cyber-attacks?

Reading this book is like embarking on a journey. You need to stay alert as every chapter contributes relevant information and insight as you approach the destination.

CHAPTER ONE

AI as a Double-Edged Sword in Cybersecurity

We encounter AI almost daily. Let's say you're a streaming freak who is always looking for the next best movies, so you choose Netflix as your streaming platform. Assuming you're a horror movie type and after seeing a few horror movies, other similar movies appear on your page, and every other recommended movie that appears is something you would like to watch. Such a prediction as to what your next choice of movie would be is almost 99% accurate. How can this platform tell if this is a particular movie you want to see? It can make these predictions because the platform AI has been programmed to think of your next choice. The AI allows you to see another movie and saves you the task of thinking about the next interesting thing. However, AI can only be as accurate as the data it gets to help it make a nearly perfect prediction. This happens not only on Netflix but on all other streaming platforms, including Facebook, YouTube, and TikTok. Perhaps you are familiar with sign-up processes just before you're onboarded on the platform; for example, you are always asked to put in an email and a password, and after that, you should log on to the next page where you need to provide your age, country/city, gender, status in some cases. Next, select your hobbies or activities you love. Finally, your account is all setup, and you will instantly start seeing some videos or reels you may prefer. Maybe at first, you would be pissed about the suggestion you get, but as you try to flip to another and then stay on the ones you prefer and watch them for a considerable amount of time, suggested videos would start aligning with your preferences.

Do you remember the details you entered when you first signed up? They are the data you have fed into the platform, and the AI uses them to think about and suggest videos according to your preference. It does this by personalizing your choices and making predictions using the data collected about you. Not only that, the more time you spend on a particular video, the more the platform uses its algorithm to learn your duration and assumes you liked it, and now it sends more of those kinds of videos to your screen. Data is the fuel that drives an AI to act with human intelligence and give you a result that you deserve or want. Thanks to the AI's machine learning capabilities.

But again, this is where it becomes more interesting. Malicious hackers also need this data to exploit and steal for nefarious reasons. So they engage in relentless and ferocious attacks to exploit any loose ends. Once they find it, they steal the data the AI Algorithm relies upon to give you a personalized experience. Even details that you are meant to see alone can be stolen. Now, what do they do with it? Well, anything! They can sell the stolen data on the dark web, where all sorts of criminals visit for money in exchange for the data. Or, the hackers might choose to use stolen data to directly create more damage. With your information in their palms, they can compromise your financial securities and steal your funds from a bank account; they can even choose to threaten you by exposing your sensitive information to the public and ask for ransom in return for not exposing it; you're a captive in their den, and as you panic, they exploit every means to drain you financially. Still, this is just one of the many data breaches or compromises most likely to happen. These hackers may even use other AI tools to study and deceive your system to give out sensitive data for further compromises.

AI today can be a necessity that has made using your devices smoother and more relaxing, and it can also be the point at which criminals can get a hold of you. It is a double-edged sword; it can be used for good and evil. Now, we must find a middle ground. A balance where one would have to enjoy all the benefits of AI and still be safe against the dark force on the other end doing everything to ruin your enjoyment and put you in a situation of perpetual regrets. AI-driven cybersecurity tools must come into the mix.

AI-driven Cybersecurity Tools

If you're a cybersecurity expert, it is understandable that you know the ropes of staying safe online. However, dealing with cyber threats can take a lot of work. Some threats might slip through right under your nose without even realizing it because you have too many on your plate to deal with. You need AI-driven cybersecurity tools to assist you in your tasks while you deal with other activities. With their machine learning capabilities, these tools can run in the system background when installed to continuously monitor and detect potential threats that could otherwise slip through any traditional cybersecurity system. This way, you're guaranteed to have an eagle eye watching over your security while you get your hands full with other tasks and ensure that nothing happens without your awareness.

Your security becomes proactive rather than reactive.

On the other hand, if you do not have cybersecurity skills but rely on basic security protocols to keep you safe online, while it keeps you safe to an appreciable extent, there is no guarantee that you will be secure everytime. Again, it would be best to have an AI-driven cybersecurity tool and basic security protocols to enhance your safety. The good thing about these tools is that they're pretty straightforward and, once installed, can run independently without needing much help. They also counter many threats that you ordinarily can't do yourself. Some of the most important functions of AI-driven cybersecurity tools include:

Security log analysis: AI tools have transformed security log analysis by leveraging their AI machine learning algorithms to analyze vast amounts of data in real time. This can detect patterns and anomalies, even ones with no threat signatures, and may be trying to breach your organization's systems. Thus, it empowers your organization to identify and swiftly respond to potential security breaches. Also, it allows your organization to detect insider threats by comprehensively analyzing users' activities across different applications and systems.

Endpoint security: More people are working remotely today, and so is the need to secure endpoints to maintain robust cybersecurity. Traditional cybersecurity tools like Antivirus and Virtual Private Networks(VPNs) use signature-based detection, which may not detect threats in real time, leaving endpoints vulnerable in the face of emerging threats. However, with AI-driven endpoint protection, you can be sure to have a more dynamic approach towards establishing your baselines of normal endpoint behavior patterns and warn as it detects any deviation accordingly. AI will help you identify potential threats and even zero-day attacks, given its constant learning of your network behavior without needing signature updates. Security teams can be empowered to enhance user account security and password protection with AI using advanced authentication methods. Having an AI-driven solution like fingerprint scanners, facial recognition, and CAPTCHA filters real from malicious login attempts.

Encryption: AI adds another layer to your security system through encryption. It does this through encryption algorithms like Secure Hash Algorithm(SHA) and Advanced Encryption Standard(AES), which are designed to be almost impossible to crack. The unique thing about this security later brought by AI is that it uses security tools and tricks that make it very difficult for any attacker or the use of another AI to predict how it works.

AI-based SIEM Tools

Before the advent of artificial intelligence, traditional Security Information and Event Management (SIEM) systems were a core component of the Security Operations Center (SOC), designed to aggregate, correlate, and analyze security data from diverse sources. By integrating logs, events, and alerts from multiple security solutions, traditional SIEMs provided SOCs with a centralized view of an organization's security posture. These tools helped detect and analyze potential threats, supporting incident response processes. However, as cyber threats have evolved and grown in complexity, so has the sheer volume of data generated across an organization's network, endpoints, and applications, rendering many legacy SIEM systems insufficient to keep pace with modern cyber risks.

Traditional SIEM systems, while invaluable, struggled with the challenge of handling large-scale, heterogeneous data sources. They often required extensive manual configuration, relied heavily on static correlation rules, and were prone to generating large volumes of false positives—creating alert fatigue among security analysts. The rapid increase in both the frequency and sophistication of cyberattacks exacerbated these issues, overwhelming SOC teams and making it challenging to identify real threats among the noise. This is where AI-based SIEM solutions step in to transform security operations by addressing the limitations of legacy systems.

The Role of AI in Enhancing SIEM Capabilities

AI-based SIEM solutions leverage artificial intelligence, machine learning, and big data analytics to enhance traditional SIEM capabilities, making them more agile, intelligent, and responsive to modern cybersecurity needs. By employing AI-driven algorithms, these solutions can ingest and analyze massive datasets in real-time, allowing them to identify patterns and detect threats that might otherwise go unnoticed. This intelligent data processing capability means that AI-based SIEM tools can predict potential threats before they escalate, adding a proactive element to cybersecurity.

One of the most transformative aspects of AI in SIEM is its ability to correlate and analyze data at a depth that surpasses human capabilities. Through machine learning, AI-based SIEM tools can recognize anomalies, behavioral changes, and subtle indicators of compromise within enormous volumes of data. For instance, rather than relying on static rules to trigger alerts (as traditional SIEM systems do), machine learning algorithms adaptively learn what constitutes 'normal' behavior within an organization's network and flag deviations that could signify malicious activity. This adaptive learning minimizes the need for manual rule-setting and reduces the likelihood of false positives, allowing security analysts to focus on genuine threats.

Furthermore, AI-driven SIEM tools offer enhanced contextual awareness, enabling them to make more nuanced assessments of potential threats. By cross-referencing data from various sources—such as user behavior analytics (UBA), threat intelligence feeds, and endpoint activity logs—AI-based SIEMs create a holistic view of an organization's security environment. This contextual intelligence enables these tools to distinguish between benign anomalies and genuine threats, drastically improving the accuracy and efficiency of threat detection.

Automating Incident Response with AI-Based SIEM

One of the most significant advantages of AI-based SIEM systems is their ability to automate incident response processes, which can greatly reduce the time between threat detection and response. In traditional security setups, analysts must often manually investigate alerts, which is time-consuming and prone to human error. In contrast, AI-enhanced SIEM solutions can automatically initiate response protocols as soon as a threat is identified, minimizing the impact of a potential security breach.

For example, if an AI-based SIEM detects an unusual login pattern or a sudden spike in data transfers from a sensitive server, it can automatically trigger predefined incident response workflows. These workflows might include actions such as isolating affected devices, blocking suspicious IP addresses, or elevating the alert to a human analyst for further review. By automating these routine response tasks, AI-based SIEM systems reduce the burden on security teams, enabling them to respond to threats faster and more efficiently.

AI-based SIEMs can also use natural language processing (NLP) to analyze incident reports and threat intelligence sources, allowing them to refine their response strategies based on new information. For instance, if a particular type of malware is known to exploit a vulnerability in certain software, an AI-based SIEM can adjust its monitoring criteria to prioritize alerts related to that software, enhancing its ability to detect similar threats in the future. This continuous learning and adaptability are key advantages of AI-based SIEM, as they allow security systems to stay relevant and responsive to evolving threat landscapes.

Real-Time Threat Intelligence and Predictive Analysis

Another crucial capability of AI-based SIEM tools is their use of predictive analytics to identify emerging threats before they become active attacks. Through the analysis of historical attack patterns, behavioral data, and real-time threat intelligence feeds, AI-based SIEM solutions can predict potential security risks, providing SOCs with advanced warnings that allow them to take preventive action.

Predictive analytics relies on sophisticated algorithms that learn from past incidents and identify patterns that may indicate a new threat vector. For instance, if a certain sequence of network activities has previously been associated with ransomware deployment, the AI-based SIEM can flag similar sequences as potential precursors to a ransomware attack, even if the specific ransomware variant has not been encountered before. This capability not only enhances threat detection but also allows security teams to proactively strengthen defenses in areas of high risk, shifting from reactive to preventive security.

In addition to predictive threat analysis, AI-based SIEMs integrate threat intelligence from external sources, such as global threat feeds, industry-specific intelligence, and indicators of compromise (IoCs) shared by other organizations. This integration enriches the SIEM's database with up-to-date information on emerging threats, which the AI algorithms can analyze in real-time to identify indicators that match known attack patterns. By correlating internal data with external threat intelligence, AI-based SIEMs enhance their situational awareness and allow organizations to respond to global threats more effectively.

Improving Efficiency and Reducing Alert Fatigue

A major challenge faced by SOCs is the phenomenon of alert fatigue, where security teams are overwhelmed by the sheer volume of alerts generated by traditional SIEM systems, many of which turn out to be false positives. This overload can lead to missed threats, as analysts become desensitized to alerts or struggle to prioritize their responses. AI-based SIEM tools address this issue by filtering out false positives and categorizing alerts based on risk level and context.

Machine learning models in AI-driven SIEM platforms continuously learn from past incidents, adjusting their algorithms to distinguish genuine threats from benign anomalies. This adaptive capability enables AI-based SIEMs to prioritize high-risk alerts, allowing security teams to focus on critical incidents while ignoring low-risk activities that do not pose a significant threat. In doing so, these tools reduce the likelihood of alert fatigue, helping security teams maintain a high level of vigilance without becoming overwhelmed.

In addition, AI-based SIEMs can automate the process of triaging alerts, using predefined criteria to assess the severity of each alert and determine appropriate response actions. For example, if an alert indicates unusual activity in an administrator account, the SIEM might prioritize it as high-risk and trigger an immediate investigation. By categorizing alerts and automating responses, AI-based SIEMs streamline SOC operations, allowing security analysts to work more efficiently and improving the overall effectiveness of security operations.

Enhancing Incident Response through Collaborative AI Systems

Modern AI-based SIEM systems are not isolated tools but part of a broader ecosystem that includes other AI-driven security solutions, such as endpoint detection and response (EDR) tools, network traffic analyzers, and cloud security platforms. By collaborating with these tools, AI-based SIEMs enhance their data collection and analysis capabilities, creating a unified and comprehensive approach to cybersecurity.

For instance, an AI-based SIEM can integrate with EDR tools to gather detailed information about endpoint activities, enabling a deeper analysis of potential threats. If a suspicious file is detected on a user's device, the SIEM can cross-reference data from the EDR tool to determine if the file exhibits characteristics associated with known malware. This collaborative approach enables AI-based SIEMs to provide more accurate threat detection and incident response by leveraging data and insights from multiple security sources.

Moreover, AI-based SIEM systems can integrate with cloud security solutions to monitor activities within cloud environments, which are increasingly vulnerable to threats. Given that many organizations now operate hybrid or multi-cloud environments, AI-driven SIEMs provide the visibility needed to detect anomalous behavior across different platforms, ensuring comprehensive security coverage. This collaboration between AI-based SIEMs and cloud security tools enhances security across an organization's entire digital infrastructure, providing SOCs with a holistic view of potential threats and vulnerabilities.

A New Era for SOCs: The Strategic Role of AI-Driven SIEM Tools

The adoption of AI-based SIEM tools signifies a new era in the field of cybersecurity, where security teams are no longer limited to reactive defenses. By enabling predictive threat detection, real-time data correlation, and automated incident response, AI-driven SIEM solutions empower SOCs to transition from a reactive to a proactive approach. These advancements have transformed SIEM from a monitoring tool into a strategic component of cybersecurity, enhancing resilience against emerging threats and improving operational efficiency.

How AI Enhances Cybersecurity

AI-driven cybersecurity tools are good countermeasures against 99% of cybersecurity threats. Several types of AI-driven cybersecurity tools exist, but they all have similar anatomy. However, some may be better suited to one particular threat against another.

So, how does an AI enhance your cybersecurity?

Threat Detection: As I mentioned earlier, all AI-driven cybersecurity tools have a similar basic anatomy. That is, they have machine learning capabilities. So, they rely on their machine learning algorithms to analyze vast data to pick up patterns that may indicate potential cyber threat(s). The AI tools use their learning abilities to study past incidents and use the acquired knowledge to detect known threats like phishing attempts, malware, and new threats never seen before in real time. According to Instinct's Chuck Everett, AI models boast 80% to 92% security rates. More than the 30% to 60% achieved by legacy signature-based malware detection systems. This AI sends feedback as a notification in case of detection, calling the attention of cybersecurity teams to do what is needed. It allows cybersecurity teams to act quicker and wade off any suspected or potential cybersecurity breaches.

Anomaly Detection: Another way AI enhances cybersecurity is anomaly detection. It does this by constantly monitoring the system's behavior patterns and flagging any deviation from the norm that could suggest a potential risk that may compromise system security, such as unusual network traffic or user activities. The AI can adapt to the evolving threat landscape with its machine learning abilities to recognize subtle patterns that are deviant from the norm in a way that traditional cybersecurity systems could likely miss.

Automation: A greater advantage that AI brings onboard cybersecurity is automation. Cybersecurity teams already have too much on their plates, and managing repetitive tasks like alerts, scanning logs for suspicious activity, and autonomously responding to low-level threats can be time-consuming if security teams do it the traditional way. The automation brought about by AI significantly cut down on human errors that are prevalent when done manually. It allows for a speedy response, giving the team plenty of time to focus and deal with tasks of higher priority and more complex. According to IBM in one of its publications, AI can reduce the time it traditionally takes to detect and respond to cybersecurity threats by 14 weeks. With an automated incident response system, cybersecurity teams can rest assured that the organization's systems can automatically quarantine and block out all suspected malicious activity in real-time, thereby reducing the impact of any attack on the systems.

Case studies of AI Successfully Thwarting Attacks.

Here are some real-life cyber security attacks that were successfully thwarted:

Threat Detection and prevention

The first case concerns threat detection and prevention. As we have seen, threat detection is an area where AI excels, and an AI-based cybersecurity system demonstrated this incredible fit with valor in thwarting threats on Honeywell's platform. With the help of AI, the platform could analyze massive data from its industrial control systems, which allowed it to identify unusual behavior or patterns indicative of cyber threats. This allows the company's system to detect and block suspicious traffic that may be trying to breach its control systems.

Behavior Analytics

Amazon's user behavior analytics is another successful AI case study in thwarting attacks. Amazon offers various AI-powered security services through its Amazon Web Service (AWS) platform, revolutionizing how businesses detect and prevent threats.

- One such example of Amazon's service is the AWS GuardDuty, which manages threat detection systems. It analyzes different data sources and includes AWS CloudTrail logs, DNS logs, and VPC Flow Logs to detect fishy patterns or behavior that could indicate a breach. It does this by identifying atypical networks, unauthorized access to sensitive data attempts, and unusual API call spikes.

- An AI-powered service offered through AWS is the AWS Inspector. It functions by continuously monitoring solutions and offering assistance in identifying security vulnerabilities within an organization's AWS infrastructure.

- Not only that, there is AWS Maci. It is an innovative offering and an all-around data security management service that uses machine learning capabilities to discover, protect, and classify sensitive data within the AWS space. Macie conducts in-depth analyses to identify vital information such as intellectual property (IP), financial data, and personally identifiable information (PII).

Advanced Threat Response

Our next successful case study is in the advanced threat response and mitigation in Wells Fargo. Deep within Wells Fargo's cybersecurity architecture is an AI-powered threat detection and response platform that employs advanced machine learning algorithms to analyze massive amounts of data, including files, email communications, and network traffic. Processing these data in real-time allows the AI system to identify patterns and abnormal behaviors that may indicate malicious threats or activities. So, as soon as a threat is present, Wells Fargo's AI system triggers a proactive response automatically, such as prompt blocking of malicious traffic or restricting suspected files from spreading across other parts of the organization's network.

Vulnerability Assessment and Management

Now, this case study is one of vulnerability assessment and management in Splunk. The Splunk Enterprise platform relies on machine learning algorithms to analyze vast amounts of data from user activity, system events, and network logs. Such an AI-driven approach enables the platform to identify abnormal patterns that may indicate a potential attack or reveal lurking vulnerabilities in real time. An advantage that Splunk's AI-driven Vulnerability Assessment and Management has over other platforms is the intelligent prioritization of threats. Therefore, by analyzing data with AI algorithms, Splunk's platform can assess the impact and severity of each vulnerability with pinpoint accuracy, giving the security team more time to deal with the most important risk quickly and efficiently.

Security Operation Automation

Let's see the fifth success case study. Here, we have security operations and automation in Plaid. Plaid uses an advanced machine learning algorithm to analyze several data points, such as security numbers, addresses, customer names, and so on, to provide background information. With the AI system, bank account identification and verification are swift and seamless. This significantly erases any room for errors or malicious activity. It also allows for a streamlined onboarding process for other financial institutions and their customers. Plaid's AI-driven platform makes any manual processes or extensive paperwork unnecessary and allows for a speedy customer onboarding process while ensuring the safety of all data assets.

Threat Intelligence and Predictive Analytics

The last successful case in thwarting threats here is the case of threat intelligence and predictive analytics in PayPal. An important application of AI in PayPal's cybersecurity strategy is in transaction analysis. Given the high volume of transactions happening on the platform daily, using manual means of scrutiny from identity potential fraud wouldn't be feasible. However, the AI's rapid processing capabilities enable it to examine each transaction for any potential red flags with high efficiency. Also, PayPal has deployed this AI to identify and block suspicious websites. As malicious attackers evolve in their ways to trick users through scam and phishing tactics, AI diligently scans the web to identify content that may carry potential risks or signs of cyber threats.

Benefits of AI in predictive analytics.

Using AI for predictive analysis has many benefits, including the potential to transform how organizations and businesses operate and make important decisions.

The first benefit you will derive from onboarding AI for your analytics is enhancing accuracy in prediction. AI algorithms that rely on the power of machine learning are capable of analyzing vast datasets more accurately than any traditional statistical model can do. They're able to detect correlations and patterns that may be overlooked as irrelevant by traditional means or even by human analysts, bringing about an accurately perfect prediction.

The next benefit is handling massive and complex data sets. AI can deal with a massive data set in split seconds, which would be too cumbersome for traditional processing tools to manage. With AI datasets, data can be quickly analyzed and interpreted from different sources without being burdened by the sheer volumes, whether from real-time streaming, images, or text, making it an invaluable tool in any organization or business.

Another benefit lies in real-time analysis and decision-making. AI can analyze vast datasets in real-time and provide prompt insights for critical decision-making. This is particularly beneficial for health care and financial industries, where split-second decisions can save lives or billions of dollars.

Yet another important benefit of AI is behavioral prediction. Learning from customer data patterns, AI can predict likely behavior shortly, such as potential churns, product or service preferences, and purchasing patterns. Such insight would guide businesses in fine-tuning their strategies for better prospects and ways to improve their customers' experience.

Now, in risk assessment and management, you can leverage AI predictive capabilities to assess your business/organization's risks. By analyzing a company's historical data, an AI can forecast any potential risk lurking in the background, allowing you to take proactive steps toward managing such risk effectively.

There are also benefits such as cost reduction and efficiency. Relying on the automated processes of predictive AI analysis renders the manual processes of data analysis needless. Manual means can be tedious, time-consuming, and costly, but with automated AI processes, there is improved efficiency of operation, which significantly cuts down on costs.

Improved product development is yet another benefit that cannot be overlooked. As AI-driven predictive analytics can tell about the product development process, businesses can leverage it to design products that are not only best suited for the market but also tailored to consumer preferences and trends.

A personalized customer experience has the benefit of being personalized. AI can develop a personalized customer experience through predictive analytics. It can predict customers' behavior and preferences, which businesses can use to increase satisfaction and loyalty.

We can't ignore the benefits of dynamic adaptation and learning, as AI models can learn and adapt to new realities continuously. This enhances predictive insights and continues to be near-accurate and relevant.

With AI predictive analytics, businesses can derive great benefits by gaining foresight into trends, opportunities, and potential challenges. This can help businesses plan strategically to meet their goals and objectives.

Our last but not least benefit is bias reduction. AI systems could undoubtedly have biases. However, advanced models being developed to identify and significantly reduce these biases will surely lead to more acceptable predictive outcomes.

AI in the Hands of Cybercriminals

AI in the hands of criminals is like a loaded gun in the hands of a child. However, the difference is that the child may assume the gun to be a toy, but the criminal is well aware of the tool in hand. While the child can be persuaded and strategically disarmed with no one hurt, there is no possible physical way to take an AI off the hands of a criminal. AI is open to all, so any talk about controlling criminals' access to it would be denying everyone, including those seeking to use it for legitimate purposes. It brings us to a crossroad. Could we all be that helpless? Imagine your financial data in the hands of malicious hackers who obtained it using an AI tool. You would be restless, and unless you do something drastic to secure whatever should be secured, every tick of the clock increases your risk of losing your life savings. That is what it means to have an AI in the hands of criminals.

If that is not serious enough, now imagine a terrorist in a faraway country successfully gaining control of the USA's intercontinental ballistic missiles using an AI tool, each armed with a kilotons of nuclear warhead. We can only imagine the outcome. An AI in the hands of a criminal is like a rebel holding a Samurai sword and must be disarmed with knowledge and tact before irreversible damage is caused.

So, how do hackers use AI to evolve attacks?

Hackers use AI to evolve attacks in four major ways:

Phishing

Our world experienced a tremendous evolution in AI after introducing writing tools like ChatGPT and Bard in 2022 and 2023. This tool has improved so much today that even inexperienced writers can write excellent marketing copies. Criminals use these tools to write a perfect email that a victim receiver can hardly tell it's a scam. Before now, phishing texts and emails were easily detected because they were often badly written. When these emails are well written, there is a greater chance that a criminal would have to convince a victim to give out sensitive information. There are an estimated 3.4 billion spam emails sent each day; it is a game of numbers. Assuming the success rate of every 3.4 billion spam emails sent each day is 30% before AI writing tools. Now, that rate would have increased to about 40%. If you do the math, you should have a significant number of people who would likely fall victim to email scams.

Automation of Interactions

Developers aim to make interaction between customers and services easier, so they provide AI tools and automated responses to optimize these interactions. Today, you're most likely to get a response from an AI before speaking with a human representative. Criminals exploit these automated responses by creating many automated interactions against their victims at an impossible scale if they were to be human.

Through these, they impersonate legitimate services such as a bank by email or mobile phone to elicit information that would give them access to their victims' money.

Deep Fakes

Today, AI can generate mathematical models that can undergo training using large numbers of real-world data, making the models better suited for a task. The deepfake technology employed in audio and video is a typical example of this situation. We have had deepfake incidents where a video surfaced online showing Simon singing opera on the America's Got Talent show. Even though this is still a far-reaching technology for most criminals, the reality remains that AI can mimic how an individual would respond to text, make phone calls, leave voice notes, and even write emails.

Brute forcing

This is another way criminals compromise their victim's systems and penetrate their accounts or systems. It happens in a way where characters and symbols are strategically tried to find any match as a password. Longer and more complex passwords are always recommended to secure your account because they would be difficult to guess or crack. The brute force method is resource-intensive, and it's easier for the criminals if they know more about the victim. That is why it is very important to keep sensitive personal, home, and office information away from the public or social media. The criminals can start with you writing down names of your favorite pet, best friends, name of close relatives, favorite food, and birthday, and when algorithms trained on your data are involved, it can help the criminals to develop a more accurate list of priorities which allows to target multiple people at a time as the resource deployed on this one would be minimal.

Improvements in AI are increasing by the day and faster than laws and regulations are established to contain its excess and abuse. It leaves room for exploitative activities to go unchecked, making systems and people more vulnerable. Who would be the next victim of a malicious cyber-attack, and do we have any countermeasures for a yet-to-be-seen threat? AI, without a doubt, is enhancing cyber-attacks beyond what humans are capable of.

CHAPTER TWO

AI-Powered Threats: A New Breed of Cyberattacks

Cyberattacks are no longer what they used to be in the past. Before now, malicious attackers used simple rule-based methods to execute attacks. That is to say, traditionally, the attackers operated in a basic 'if-then' routine, and if the answer to their question "Is this a target?" was a 'yes,' then execute malicious code, but if 'No,' then move on. The traditional malicious attacks took a predictable, straightforward, and detectable path. However, this began to change when cybercriminals realized that cybersecurity experts had caught up with their tricks, using sandboxes and other forms of defense. So they decided to change their game and swapped what was initially a simple tactic to something far more sophisticated through AI exploits.

AI has become a powerful tool in the hands of cybercriminals today. It gives attackers the leverage to carry out attacks that do not depend on following basic instructions but use an advanced learning method instead. Now, think of a cyber attack with a mind of its own; that is how far AI attacks have come. With Deep Neural Networks (DNN), these attacks can adapt their behavior according to what is learned from each activity. That is to say, the rigid 'if-then' kind of execution is out of the way, and executable attacks can think independently, make decisions based on information they acquire, and cause far-reaching damages while evading detection. AI has given attackers a tool that learns and adapts, helping them more efficiently search and find vulnerabilities in real-time, rendering traditional defenses incapable of detecting malicious attacks.

The threat level in an AI-driven cyberattack goes beyond minor disruption or data theft. Such attacks can be more serious and life-threatening. As we have seen, they come with financial consequences and erode trust.

A typical example of an AI tool that attackers use is PassGAN. The PassGAN AI tool is designed to generate password guesses quickly to bypass traditional cybersecurity systems. These kinds of attacks are not just a random guessing exercise. Instead, they gain insights to become smarter and more precise while bypassing set protocols put in place to access protected systems without being detected. An AI-exploited attack like PassGAN exposes even robust defense systems to an intelligent and evolving threat.

Hackers are breaking into vulnerable systems, learning, analyzing, and adapting maneuvers. They employ AI to study and learn reliable patterns in the system to exploit weaknesses without triggering the traditional cybersecurity systems set in place to secure them. The attack is often undetectable because they can mimic trusted features, which could make their actions appear legitimate as they try to find existing vulnerabilities to exploit. What makes it all the scarier is that it doesn't just happen once when they strike. These AI-driven exploits evolve as situations change, learning from failed attempts and refining tactics to come back in a more robust attempt.

The evolving capabilities of AI attacks are a nightmare for most cybersecurity teams. Given their speed and complexity, they are a significant challenge for any human team to deal with effectively. The evolving nature of these attacks makes static defenses inadequate. Therefore, defending against these AI-driven threats is now a race against time, a battle between machine efficiency and human limitations. Cybersecurity teams must strategize beyond what is obtainable in traditional tools and static defenses.

The rise of machine-speed attacks has also transformed the cybersecurity outlook. Before now, cyber threats were executed at human speeds; a hacker finds a target, prepares for an attack, and launches the attack. But today, AI and machine learning have helped cybercriminals improve their ways, ushering in a new wave of highly automated and incredibly fast attacks that launch, adapt, and evolve in seconds. This significant shift, like cyberattacks, calls organizations to rethink their cybersecurity approach in defending digital assets and staying ahead of the game of cybercriminals.

Also, AI aids in scaling attacks. It makes it possible for malicious attackers to launch attacks on a massive scale and target multiple systems simultaneously. Previously, this scale of attack required extensive coordination, time, and resources. But here, a single command can activate several attacks on multiple systems spread across different targets with AI-driven automation. For example, a malicious attacker can deploy an AI-powered bot to carry out brute-force attacks on multiple systems at a go, overwhelming existing defenses. Instead of using a simple single-point intrusion for your cybersecurity approach, you need to use a cybersecurity approach that includes tools and practices capable of responding effectively to multiple threats simultaneously. Still, AI can serve positively in helping to identify vulnerabilities in ways that far exceed human capabilities, and this has revolutionized our cybersecurity landscape such that it gives organizations the ability to counter AI exploits faster.

Using static tools and traditional cybersecurity strategies can be time-consuming as they often require cybersecurity teams to rely on manual audits and analysis. Cybersecurity experts must painstakingly scan code network architectures and configurations to identify weaknesses. This strategy is not only slow but more prone to human errors. However, cybersecurity teams can leverage AI, which comes with advanced algorithms, to automate the vulnerability identification process, which is significantly faster and more efficient than traditional methods. According to experts in the cybersecurity industry, AI systems can analyze vast amounts of data and accurately identify vulnerabilities in split seconds or minutes, which may take human analysts days or weeks to uncover potential security lapses.

The ability of AI to process and analyze data at scale means it can identify patterns and anomalies that may indicate vulnerability accurately. For example, machine learning algorithms can continuously monitor user behavior and network traffic and flag any unusual activity that could signify a potential security threat. Such a proactive monitoring posture allows for the quicker detection of vulnerabilities, which enables organizations to prioritize risks based on severity. Not all vulnerabilities are equal; some may pose far more risks than others. So, knowing which to address first can improve an organization's security posture significantly.

The AI's speed in identifying potential vulnerabilities is due to its ability to learn from previous incidents. Therefore, machine learning models can be trained on historical attack data to recognize which vulnerabilities were exploited in those breach incidents. That's to say, an AI can prioritize its search for vulnerabilities according to previous attack patterns. Such predictive capabilities can help organizations stay ahead of potential threats and allow them to fortify their defenses before an attack happens.

Another important part of AI's ability to identify vulnerabilities is its continuous assessment of systems activities. Given the evolving nature of the cybersecurity landscape, a static security strategy can quickly become obsolete. However, with AI, systems can perform real-time assessments by continuously scanning the organization's systems for new vulnerabilities that may arise during software updates or when a new application is installed. This form of constant vigilance is essential for modern organizations hungry for new technologies in the face of dynamic cyber threats. AI ensures that defenses remain robust and effective through its continuous vulnerability identification.

Integrating AI in vulnerability management goes beyond detection. It also allows you to prioritize your organization's vulnerabilities according to the impact of a potential exploit. For example, suppose an AI cybersecurity system identifies a vulnerability affecting a critical part of your organization's system with access to sensitive data. In that case, it can alert the security team to make priorities for remediating that issue. Such prioritization is very important when resources are limited, allowing the security team to direct a greater effort in eliminating critical threats.

Furthermore, AI can give your organization insights into how cybercriminals might exploit vulnerabilities. It does this by simulating potential attack scenarios. This allows the security team to understand better the possible implications of a vulnerability and how malicious attackers might capitalize on them to gain unauthorized access or exfiltrate critical data. The information gained from these insights can help your organization make informed decisions about developing or implementing its cybersecurity strategies.

The incredibly fast pace at which AI helps identify vulnerabilities would help your organization greatly reduce its window of exposure to potential attacks. The faster vulnerabilities are discovered and remediated, the less time cybercriminals would have to exploit those loopholes. Research has shown that this can dramatically lower the chances of successful breaches, as malicious attackers mostly rely on exploiting known vulnerabilities that may not have been remediated or patched.

But, while we celebrate the AI's impressive speed and efficiency in identifying vulnerabilities, we must remember that these systems are not infallible. Yes, AI should be used to complement human expertise and not to replace it. While it is agreed that AI can automate several tasks and give valuable insights, human analysts are still needed to interpret results, understand the context of a vulnerability, and make strategic decisions about mitigation or remediation.

Deepfake as a Cyber Threat

One of the challenges we face in advancements in artificial intelligence is deepfakes. But what are deepfakes? To answer that, they are AI-generated media in which a person's likeness, be it their voice or face or both, is digitally manipulated to create a realistic but entirely fake representation. Deepfakes are sophisticated forms of digital deception capable of posing significant risks to individuals and businesses. They were initially perceived as a novelty in digital media, and today, they have evolved into cybersecurity threats of great concern. The efficiency and accuracy with which they imitate behaviors, appearances, and voices have led to misuse across various sectors, from corporate espionage to financial fraud. These highly realistic but alterly fake representations are created using machine learning algorithms, particularly deep learning techniques. Deepfakes rely on datasets such as audio, photos, and video files to mimic individual voices or appearances almost perfectly. The process is commonly carried out using Generative Adversarial Networks (GANs), with a part of its algorithm generating the fake content and another evaluating its realism and, as a result, improving output with every alteration.

While deepfakes were originally popular in the entertainment industry, where the faces of celebrities were altered in videos, their application has gone beyond these borders. Given the prevalence of open-source deepfake AI tools and software, they are now accessible to all who possess basic computer skills. What was initially a niched specialized skill has become widely available, making deepfakes more prevalent and difficult to control.

Now let's see how deepfakes could pose a new business threat:

Corporate espionage and fraud

The potential for corporate espionage is one of the most alarming risks deepfakes pose to businesses. Imagine yourself being an executive and slated for a high-ranking official to appear to participate in a confidential discussion on a highly sensitive topic concerning your organization, only for an entire audio or video recording to be fabricated. Cybercriminals can capitalize on these fabricated clips, damage corporate reputation, manipulate stock prices, and extract proprietary information. Regarding financial fraud, deepfakes are increasingly applied and used in vishing. Vishing is a voice phishing attack, and malicious attackers can use it to impersonate a company or business executive—for instance, a scammer sounding like the CEO can deceive employees into approving unauthorized transactions. There are recorded cases of this kind of incident, and it has caused businesses to lose huge sums of money to criminals.

Social engineering and identity theft

Cybercriminals can weaponize deepfakes in social engineering attacks by manipulating business partners or employees while impersonating trusted figures. For instance, an attacker can create voice recordings or videos of familiar faces, such as senior managers, to manipulate employees into disclosing sensitive information or to gain unauthorized access to systems. Regarding identity theft, attackers can use deepfakes to bypass facial recognition security systems by presenting a realistic fake image or video. They could compromise access to restricted areas or physical locations, leaving organizations vulnerable to impactful losses.

Brand and Reputation Damage

Damaging content can be created using deepfakes and quickly go viral on social media, resulting in reputation harm and severe brand. For instance, one can create a deepfake video showing a CEO making offensive remarks or shown in a video displaying unethical behavior; it can spread quickly and lead to negative publicity, a loss of consumer confidence or trust, and a sharp decline in stock value. Even when such a video is eventually proven to be fake, the damage already done to that brand's reputation would be difficult to reverse, especially at a time when information travels faster.

Market manipulation and financial impact

Some malicious market speculators are finding deepfakes handy. Deepfakes videos can be strategically released to manipulate stock prices or affect market sentiment. So these cheats often release fake videos of a CEO announcing financial distress or product failure, which could lead to a fall in stock prices, even if that company quickly goes on air to debunk such. As for companies with high trading volumes, this can lead to a significant financial loss, impacting employees, shareholders, and the large market.

Legal and compliance concern

Businesses can suffer legal troubles due to deepfakes regarding data privacy regulations and compliance. Governments worldwide are working hard to understand and legislate against the deepfake menace, and businesses can get caught up in the middle as they may be found liable, especially when they fail to implement proper safeguards against threats posed by deepfakes. Also, companies that fall victim to deepfakes may face challenges in proving that such content is not authentic, which could lead to prolonged legal disputes and potential fines.

Some real-life examples of deepfake usage in fraud and cyber espionage include the following:

The first is about three Canadian men tricked into watching deepfake videos of Prime Minister Justin Trudeau and Space X boss Elon Musk. These men fell for the trick, believing the videos were real, and decided to invest $373,000 of their money, which they lost to the scammers.

Another deepfake case was on a British engineering company, Arup. Arup was a victim of deepfake fraud. The scammers tried to trick the company's employees into sending HK$ 200 million, about 20 million Euros, using an artificial intelligence-generated video call. According to the Hong Kong police, in February, a worker of an unnamed company was tricked into sending a vast amount of money by individuals on a hoax call while posing as a senior manager in this company. Arup confirmed that the company was involved early in the year and had to inform the Hong Kong police about the incident. It also confirmed fake images and voices were used.

The next case involves a finance worker at a multinational firm. According to the Hong Kong police, the worker was tricked into transferring $25 million to fraudsters who posed as the company's chief financial officer using deepfake technology during a video conference call.

Hong Kong police said during a briefing that the elaborate scam involved the worker being duped into attending a video call with what he thought were several other staff members, all of whom were, in fact, deepfake recreations.

The senior deputy superintendent, Barun Chan Shun-ching, told TTHK, the city public broadcaster, that everyone in the multi-person video conference was fake.

The deputy superintendent went on to say that initially, the worker grew suspicious after he received a message that was thought to be from the UK-based company's chief financial officer. So, the worker suspected a phishing email as she realized it was about carrying out a secret transaction.

But these doubts were shattered after a video call. Chan added that other people attending the video call conference appeared and sounded like well-recognized colleagues.

After being convinced by the fake video conference, the worker agreed to send $200 million, which is about 25.6 million. The worker only discovered it was all fake after the employee checked with the firm's head office.

Still, the Hong Kong deputy police superintendent, Chan, also related a case involving eight stolen identity cards that were all reported stolen by the owners. These identities were used to make 90 loan applications and over 50 bank account registrations in a short space between July and September 2023. The police also said that AI deepfakes had been used on at least 20 occasions to trick facial recognition programs with identity card imitations.

Even the president of the United States was not spared of deepfakes when the democratic political consultant used a robocall that used AI to impersonate President Biden. The Federal Communication Commission sued Steve Kramer to face a federal fine and criminal charge for that act. He was slammed with a $6 million fine after admitting to the fake call sent to thousands of people in New Hampshire.

As deepfake and other AI-generated media evolve, identifying these digital manipulations has become increasingly complex. At the same time, detection technology advances, and distinguishing authentic content from a sophisticated AI-generated fake is challenging.

Now, let's examine the challenges in detecting AI-generated content and what it means for you and your business.

Rapidly Advancing Technology

AI technology is constantly improving, which means that each generation of deepfake tools becomes more advanced than the last. When you consider how quickly these technologies progress, detection tools are often one step behind. New versions with enhanced realism are released as researchers develop methods to detect a certain type of deepfake. This constant race makes it challenging for businesses to rely on any single detection tool for long-term security.

Increased Accessibility and Democratization of AI Tools

Today, anyone with an internet connection can access deepfake software and other AI-driven media creation tools. This widespread accessibility has led to a rise in sophisticated fake content creation by people with limited technical skills. The democratization of these tools also means that you're facing an ever-growing volume of AI-generated content, making it difficult to identify every instance of manipulated media, especially if you don't have a dedicated team focused on content verification.

Lifelike Precision and Improved Quality

Modern AI algorithms produce content that is increasingly difficult to distinguish from reality. For instance, deepfake videos now include subtle facial expressions, synchronized lip movements, and other nuanced details that mimic real behavior. Even when examining these details closely, it can be hard to spot inconsistencies. This precision makes it easier for malicious actors to deceive even trained eyes, meaning you need advanced technology to catch subtle cues that would otherwise go unnoticed.

Inconsistencies in Detection Tools

AI detection tools are not foolproof. Many detection algorithms rely on analyzing patterns and inconsistencies, but these tools can sometimes produce false positives, mistakenly flagging authentic content as fake. This inconsistency can create challenges for businesses like yours that need reliable verification methods. In high-stakes scenarios, such as legal cases or public statements, false positives could damage trust and credibility. As a result, detection tools must be paired with human oversight and other validation methods, but even then, complete accuracy is difficult to achieve.

Challenges in Audio Deepfake Detection

While most discussions around deepfakes focus on video content, audio deepfakes are also a serious threat. Audio deepfakes can mimic voices accurately, making them extremely difficult to detect. Identifying manipulated audio could be a serious challenge if your business relies on voice authentication or voice-based interactions. Current detection tools need help with the complexity of synthesized voice patterns, especially when malicious actors use high-quality audio recordings to train their models.

Limited Resources for Small to Medium Businesses

Investing in advanced AI detection technology can be costly. For smaller businesses, the expenses associated with state-of-the-art detection software, specialized training, or hiring cybersecurity experts may be challenging. This financial barrier creates a gap in security between large organizations with dedicated resources and smaller businesses that may need help to keep up. Without the resources to verify content thoroughly, your business could be more vulnerable to deepfake-related risks, such as fraud or reputational harm.

Lack of Standardized Detection Protocols

As the landscape of AI-generated content continues to evolve, standardized detection protocols remain limited. While some industry organizations work on universal standards, the field needs consistent benchmarks for detecting and authenticating content across platforms. This lack of standardization can leave you without clear guidelines for evaluating content authenticity. Without established protocols, determining the legitimacy of AI-generated content can become a complex, subjective process.

Psychological and Perceptual Bias

Human perception can sometimes work against you when evaluating potentially manipulated media. Studies show that people tend to believe information that aligns with their biases, making them more susceptible to well-crafted deepfakes. When faced with highly realistic AI-generated content, people may unconsciously trust what they see or hear, especially if it reinforces preconceived notions.

This natural bias complicates the detection process and underscores the need for rigorous, unbiased verification systems to counter our inherent trust in what appears authentic.

AI in Cyber Espionage

Artificial intelligence has so far not only become a transformative tool for businesses and individuals, but it has also become a powerful weapon in the hands of those engaged in cyber espionage. Nation-states and large organizations leverage AI to conduct sophisticated attacks, often categorized as advanced persistent threats (APTs) against perceived rivals or enemies. These AI-powered methods have successfully allowed attackers to bypass traditional security defenses, making it critical for you and your organization to have a snitch idea about such emerging threats and their possible implications.

Advanced persistent threats (APTs) are often prolonged and highly targeted attacks that aim to infiltrate and exfiltrate sensitive information from high-value targets over time. Unlike simple malware attacks, APTs are perfectly planned and carefully executed and involve continuous surveillance and adaptation to evade detection. When AI is introduced into APTs, the threat level spikes significantly.

However, AI-driven surveillance tools add another layer of complexity to the cyber espionage landscape, making it even more challenging for organizations to secure their networks. As AI is used in conducting real-time monitoring, tracking user behavior, and analyzing large datasets, attackers can gather detailed information that could be weaponized against your organization. Now, let's see how AI-powered surveillance tools are impacting cybersecurity:

1. Through Facial Recognition and Biometric Data Collection: AI-powered facial recognition has become a standard tool for surveillance in most public spaces, but it also poses significant privacy and security risks. Attackers can capitalize on these technologies to gather data on individuals within your organization by linking faces to specific roles, access privileges, or behaviors. For instance, AI surveillance cameras can track employees' movement patterns, accurately capturing entry points and locations where sensitive data may be accessed. These insights enable attackers to build detailed plans to infiltrate and extract, targeting vulnerable spots within your security infrastructure.

2. Through Behavioral Analytics and Anomaly Detection: AI-powered behavioral analytics tools can identify patterns within your organization's digital environment, such as the

number of login times, frequency with which files are accessed, and communication trends. Attackers can use this information to design attacks that align with expected behaviors, which could make unauthorized access harder to detect. Suppose your organization has established patterns for accessing certain files at specific times. In that case, AI-driven attackers can time their data exfiltration to match these patterns, allowing them to operate under the radar of anomaly detection systems.

3. Through Data Mining and Analysis of Publicly Available Information: Knowing that AI tools can mine vast amounts of publicly available data, collecting insights about an organization and its employees. Information gathered from public records, social media, and even employee LinkedIn profiles can be compiled to link all the dots, access privileges, and roles within the organization. Attackers

can use this data to map out your company's structure, identifying each individual with valuable access or potential weak spots that can be exploited through social engineering or phishing.

4. Through AI-Enabled Network Mapping and Vulnerability Scanning: Highly effective network mapping and vulnerability scanning are possible with AI-powered surveillance tools. Attackers can analyze your network's topology and identify the best paths for infiltration, looking for weak endpoints, unpatched systems, or outdated software. Therefore, using AI to scan for vulnerabilities continuously would allow attackers to adapt their strategies based on your cybersecurity updates and defense mechanisms to exploit newly identified weaknesses as soon as they appear.

5. Through Compromising Internet of Things (IoT) Devices: IoT devices, such as security cameras, smart locks, and temperature sensors, are often part of corporate networks, but these things may need more robust security. Attackers can exploit vulnerabilities in these devices to gain entry into your network, bypassing established traditional cybersecurity. Once they find their way in, they can use IoT devices as entry points to access sensitive data or deploy malware that spreads across your organization's infrastructure. The vast amount of data generated by IoT devices also provides additional insights into employee activities, network structure, and physical security, which can still be useful for attackers planning and executing further attacks.

CHAPTER THREE

Challenges in AI-based Cyber Defense Systems

The advent of artificial intelligence (AI) is shaking up the present world, revolutionizing business, transforming healthcare, enhancing financial systems, and strengthening security. The fantastic input of AI cannot be overstated. However, as AI grows, a critical concern emerges: privacy. Here's how it happens. AI needs large amounts of data to learn and improve. As a result, AI mainly relies on personal, medical, or financial information to understand and recognize patterns, refine decisions, and become more accurate. This unavoidable need for data creates a dilemma—how can we keep personal data safe, seeing AI needs so much of it?

The Intersection of Data Privacy and AI

There's almost no separating AI systems from their need for vast datasets to work effectively. For instance, there's Machine learning, a type of AI that thrives on data like personal records, browsing habits, or even health information. That is how AI can improve, adapt, and provide insights. While it seems awesome, this reliance on large datasets has a downside because it creates vulnerabilities that risk personal privacy.

IBM's 2024 Cost of a Data Breach Report showed that data breaches have continued to rise, regardless of advanced AI security measures. Funny enough, the same AI tools designed to protect data are sometimes the reason behind newer vulnerabilities. The irony leaves many businesses and security leaders puzzled. They face the challenge of balancing AI's powerful capabilities with the responsibility to protect individual privacy. It's more like managing Frankenstein!

The Vulnerabilities of Massive Data in AI Training

You see, the more data AI systems consume, the greater we risk sensitive information being exposed. There are tons of ways this exposure can happen. Some include but are not limited to data leaks, poor handling, or even using unauthorized AI tools. One example of this problem is what the experts call "*shadow AI.*" Shadow AI happens when employees use AI tools without the approval of the IT departments. Sometimes, this shadow AI happens with employees because these tools make their work easier or faster. With proper care, these sensitive data might end up in tools that have essential security measures.

For instance, generative AI tools can produce text, images, or code, but if used without supervision, they could process confidential information in unsafe environments. Research shows that nearly 40% of companies face significant pressure from business partners to adopt AI quickly. Oftentimes, this quick AI adoption only partially considers privacy risks. As a result, vulnerabilities and accidental data sharing in non-secure AI models are overlooked, exacerbating privacy concerns.

Legal and Ethical Concerns with AI Handling Sensitive Data

The legal framework around AI and data privacy is complex and rapidly evolving. Regulating bodies like the General Data Protection Regulation (GDPR) in Europe and the California Consumer Privacy Act (CCPA) in the United States ensure responsible data handling. These laws require transparency, consent, and the authority to know or delete personal data.

The problem is that AI poses unique challenges to these laws. AI systems process data to learn and make predictions. As a result, they treat data as raw material without a clear record of how each piece is used. For example, if an AI is trained on sensitive medical records, it might predict health trends without clearly revealing how it arrived at these conclusions. This lack of absolute information transparency, known as the "black box" issue, makes ensuring compliance with privacy laws difficult.

According to the European Data Protection Board, studies show that around 58% of companies need help ensuring that their AI systems meet GDPR requirements. This challenge is based on the complexity of fusing AI capabilities with legal and ethical standards for protecting personal data.

Balancing Innovation with Privacy

Despite these roadblocks, there is no denying that AI offers tremendous benefits. Many business leaders believe that AI is as revolutionary as the internet itself. In a recent survey, 84% of Chief Information Officers (CIOs) said AI would be critical for business success. However, there is still a significant need to exercise caution, as around 67% of CIOs are taking a slower approach to adopting AI due to massive security and privacy concerns.

This cautious approach demonstrates the importance of a solid foundation. To wrap it up, companies allocate more budgets toward data management than AI adoption. Businesses are investing up to four times more in data governance, ensuring they have the right protections before fully embracing AI. Security and privacy management have become inseparable from AI development. Companies prioritize compliance with privacy laws and integrating explainable AI tools to create and sustain transparency.

Mitigating Data Privacy Risks in AI Systems

To reduce the risks associated with using data in AI, security leaders and CIOs are implementing several key strategies, which include but are not limited to:

Data Minimization: This principle involves collecting only the minimum data necessary for AI to function. By reducing the data collected, companies lower the risk of breaches. Some companies also anonymize or pseudonymize data. This means changing personal details into untraceable forms to protect actual individual identities.

Transparency and Consent: Many companies are working to inform users about how their data will be used, especially in AI systems. Organizations seek user consent to comply with local privacy laws and ensure data collection meets regulations. This way, users are more in control of what and how much personal information they release to these tools.

Implementing AI Governance: Establishing strong AI governance is critical to responsible and ethical AI usage. This includes establishing policies that insist on regular audits of AI models to check data usage and privacy compliance.

Regular Security Audits: Regularly conducting security audits helps identify potential data handling weaknesses. These audits examine everything from unauthorized tools to data handling processes to ensure they meet established security standards.

Using Explainable AI: Companies are investing in explainable AI models to understand how decisions are made within AI systems. This transparency helps organizations verify that the AI complies with legal standards and ethical guidelines while providing insight into how sensitive data is used. This way, no one is left in the dark about how their data is used.

Ethical Concerns: The Social Impact of AI on Privacy

Beyond the legal implications, AI's role in society continues to raise more questions, one of which is ethical. Since AI systems rely heavily on personal data, they have the power to shape important decisions, from healthcare to advertising and so on. This enormous influence brings up questions about fairness and autonomy. Now, people wonder if AI respects individual rights and treats all users fairly.

One fundamental ethical concern is that AI-driven decisions might reinforce biases found in training data. Here's what we mean: if AI is trained on biased data, it could produce unfair or discriminatory outcomes based on its training. In cybersecurity, certain biases can lead to "over-policing" certain types of users while neglecting others who might even be a bigger threat. A 2022 MIT Study shows that biased AI, due to their training, has an error rate almost three times higher for minority groups in certain applications.

In the U.S., companies are increasingly aware of the ethical challenges posed by AI. Therefore, a balanced approach is essential, one that respects privacy and fairness while harnessing AI's potential for innovation. Ensuring that AI systems align with ethical values is becoming a priority as organizations strive to maintain consumer trust and transparency.

Bias and False Positives in AI Algorithms

As AI systems become more essential in cybersecurity, they bring amazing benefits and tough challenges. One major concern is the bias within AI algorithms, which can affect how accurately these systems detect and respond to threats. The thing is, Bias in AI not only weakens the effectiveness of cybersecurity but can lead to serious issues like false positives and negatives. This situation refers to a scenario where safe actions are flagged as threats, creating chances to miss the real threats. Both mistakes disrupt the flow of cybersecurity operations. As a result, it becomes crucial to understand and reduce bias in AI models.

This section will look at different types of bias in AI systems, how these biases arise, and their impact on cybersecurity. We will also consider practical strategies for reducing the effects of false positives and negatives on security measures.

Sources of Bias in AI

We can only forestall AI biases by truly understanding them. Essentially, AI biases involve systematic errors that lead to unfair or unequal treatment in decision-making. In cybersecurity, a biased AI model might misinterpret a harmless action as a threat or overlook a real one, which can put a system at risk. There are three primary sources of AI bias: data bias, algorithm bias, and user bias. Understanding these biases will enable us to create fairer, more accurate cybersecurity tools.

Data Bias

Data bias happens when incomplete, skewed, or insufficiently represented data is used to train an AI model. For instance, the AI system could become biased if the data lacks diversity or includes errors. In cybersecurity, this can mean that the AI model might be trained on data that doesn't cover a wide range of threats or user behaviors. As a result of this limitation, AI can be less effective in spotting threats across different settings.

Here's a thought experiment: Imagine an AI system trained mainly on malware data from a particular country. It might miss new types of threats in other regions because the training data didn't cover them. This lack of diverse data can result in the system overlooking real dangers (false negatives) or flagging safe actions as risky (false positives). To corroborate this information, a 2022 survey by the Ponemon Institute revealed that around 55% of companies reported that data bias in AI models caused operational challenges in cybersecurity.

Algorithm Bias

Algorithm/Algorithmic bias is another type of bias that arises from how the algorithms are designed or programmed. It is more like a manufacturing or design problem. This bias can be caused by assumptions made during the development of the AI model. For example, if a cybersecurity algorithm is set up to prioritize detecting certain types of attacks, like phishing, it might miss others, like zero-day vulnerabilities. That's because it is not ingrained in the algorithm to do so.

Algorithmic bias can also happen when the AI model doesn't fully consider complex data patterns, leading to incorrect predictions. Again, in cybersecurity, this can mean that some network activities get flagged too often while others are ignored. This bias can result in certain users or behaviors being wrongly labeled as security threats. A 2023 study found that around 68% of cybersecurity AI models showed signs of algorithmic bias, increasing false positives.

User Bias

User bias arises from the people who interact with the AI system, whether they know it or not. This bias can be introduced when security teams label data for AI training or feed specific types of information into the system. For instance, if a security team believes that certain user groups are more likely to pose insider threats, they might label data that reflects this bias. As a result, the AI model might learn to target these groups and flag them out unfairly.

User bias can also happen when the AI system doesn't consider diverse user behaviors. Doing so creates a model that disproportionately flags activities from certain regions or industries. In 2023, a survey of cybersecurity professionals revealed that around 43% noticed instances where their biases may have influenced AI predictions. This led to a need for retraining AI systems to ensure fairness.

Types of AI Biases in Cybersecurity

Here's a quick tabular breakdown of the common AI biases in cybersecurity:

Types of AI Biases	Description	Examples
Data Bias	Data bias occurs due to skewed or insufficient data for AI model training	AI models trained solely with U.S.-based information will likely miss threats from other regions.
Algorithmic Bias	Results from an error in the algorithm during the AI design or creation	An AI model designed by the algorithm to prioritize phishing attacks will likely ignore vulnerabilities due to zero-day attacks.
User Bias	That is due to external biases introduced to the AI by the team working with it throughout its operational life	A security team might classify activities from other user groups as a threat based on biased notions.

The Impact of Bias on Threat Detection

Now that we have understood the different AI biases, we must consider how these biases influence or affect threat detection. AI bias can seriously affect cybersecurity, especially considering how threats are identified and managed. When AI models are biased, their ability to detect and respond to security threats can be compromised.

This bias can lead to two primary issues:

1. False positives, where safe actions are flagged as threats.
2. False negatives, where real threats go unnoticed.

Both outcomes can inherently disrupt cybersecurity efforts and lead to significant operational issues

False Positives

We can liken a false positive to a false alarm. It happens when an AI system mistakenly labels an ordinarily harmless action as a security risk.

In cybersecurity, this can mean stuff like flagging safe activities. A good example would be an employee working late and accessing sensitive files flagged as suspicious. These misjudgments can lead to unnecessary investigations and overwhelm the security team with non-critical issues, draining the team of sufficient energy to handle actual security threats.

False positives bring several challenges to them. They include but are not limited to:

- **Wasted Resources**: Security teams might spend several productive hours investigating actions that later turn out to be safe. This time could be better used on actual security threats.
- **Operational Delays**: Too many false alarms can slow down business

activities. Regular tasks are disrupted for security checks.

- **Alert Fatigue**: When security teams are overburdened with false positives, they may need to pay attention to alerts. This can lead to overlooking real threats when they arise.

- **Increased Costs**: Managing an overload of false positives is expensive. More resources are required to deal with these alerts, adding to the expense of maintaining a cybersecurity team.

According to a report by the Ponemon Institute, around 40% of cybersecurity professionals experience "alert fatigue," where constant false alarms make it hard for them to stay focused on actual threats. This fatigue can make a security system less effective with time.

False Negatives

Conversely, false negatives are missed threats or situations where the AI needs to flag actual security risks. This type of error can be particularly dangerous in cybersecurity. When threats continuously go undetected, attackers have more time to exploit system vulnerabilities, increasing the risk of serious breaches.

False negatives lead to several severe consequences, which include but are not limited to:

- **Undetected Breaches**: A breach that is missing a real threat can go unnoticed for days or weeks, giving attackers prolonged access to sensitive information.
- **Compliance Risks**: Companies are often required by law to maintain certain

security standards. Missing a threat could mean failing to meet these requirements, resulting in penalties or fines.

- **Damage to Reputation**: High-profile breaches, especially those caused by missed threats, can harm a company's reputation. As a result, customers may lose trust, which can be hard to rebuild.

- **Financial Losses**: Data theft, ransomware attacks, and other breaches from undetected threats can cause companies to lose millions. In 2023, the average cost of a data breach reached $4.45 million globally, highlighting the financial risks associated with cybersecurity lapses.

As companies and businesses depend on AI to detect and handle security threats, biases that lead to false negatives in AI can have a lasting impact. An analysis by Accenture in 2023 found that companies experiencing frequent false negatives were 30% more likely to suffer data breaches than those with accurate AI models.

Therefore, understanding and addressing false positives and negatives is essential for effective cybersecurity. As AI plays a bigger role in threat detection, finding ways to reduce bias and improve accuracy will become increasingly important.

Adversarial AI: Growing Threats and Defense Strategies

As AI becomes a cornerstone in our society, from driving cars to diagnosing diseases, a new threat emerges—adversarial AI. This security threat is unique in the sense that it does not target the weaknesses of traditional software. Instead, it exploits the learning processes of most AI models. As a result, researchers and organizations are in the quest to understand these risks and develop ways to defend against them. The first step in the right direction would be understanding what adversarial Machine learning is.

What is Adversarial Machine Learning?

Adversarial machine learning is a tactic for executing security threats where the attackers feed AI systems harmful or misleading data. This harmful or misleading data is known as "adversarial examples." The essence is to coerce the system into making mistakes. These examples are subtle, usually imperceptible to humans, yet sufficiently powerful to mislead the AI. For instance, a small change to an image could trick an AI into thinking a stop sign is a yield sign. Similarly, tweaks to a sentence could cause a natural language AI to misunderstand its meaning.

The concept thrives on exploiting how AI models learn. Machine learning models are trained on large datasets to recognize patterns and make predictions. This allows attackers to manipulate input data, altering the AI's decisions and predictions in undesirable ways. The potential impact is vast, especially in critical areas like self-driving cars, medical diagnostics, and financial systems.

How Adversarial AI Manipulates Models

Although the process of adversarial AI manipulation is a complex one, it can be broken down into four main stages:

Understanding the Target System: Attackers study the AI model and analyze its algorithms, data sources, and decision logic. They might even reverse-engineer the model to identify vulnerabilities and find weaknesses to exploit. The trick here is that the better they understand the model, the more precisely they can craft adversarial inputs.

Crafting Adversarial Inputs: Attackers can create adversarial examples by understanding how the AI system works. They are specific inputs designed to fool the AI. These examples are usually subtle, sometimes as little as adjusting a few pixels in an image, yet they can mislead the model into wrong conclusions. For instance, changing small aspects of a picture could cause a self-driving car's AI to mistake a pedestrian for an object.

Exploiting the AI Model: Once the adversarial examples are ready, attackers use them to manipulate the AI, compelling it to make incorrect decisions. This manipulation can bypass security protocols or create incorrect outputs, like classifying a restricted item as harmless. Since AI processes data quickly, the damage from a successful attack could be swift and widespread.

Post-Attack Consequences: The consequences of adversarial AI attacks depend on the application. A minor error might mean misclassifying an object in a photo, but in high-stakes cases like medical diagnostics, the misclassification could lead to severe outcomes, even endangering lives. This range of possible damages highlights the importance of securing AI from adversarial threats.

Types of Adversarial Attacks

Now that we have covered what adversarial attacks are and how they operate. It's time to look at the types in action. That said, there are several types of adversarial attacks, each posing unique challenges to AI security:

White-Box vs. Black-Box Attacks: In white-box attacks, attackers fully know the AI model's inner workings, including its algorithms, structure, and training data. This inside knowledge makes for highly precise adversarial inputs. However, in black-box attacks, the attacker lacks detailed information and relies on trial and error to probe weaknesses. Irrespective of the limited access, skilled attackers can still deceive AI systems in black-box scenarios by observing and testing responses.

Evasion Attacks: These attacks thrive by deceiving AI into ignoring real threats by introducing manipulated inputs that evade detection. Evasion attacks can come in two forms:

- **Non-targeted attacks**: The goal of non-targeted attacks is to make the AI produce an incorrect result. For example, an AI identifying traffic signs might fail to recognize a stop sign due to slight modifications, leading to a dangerous situation on the road.

- **Targeted attacks**: Targeted attacks have specific outcomes, like forcing an AI to categorize a threat as non-threatening. In cybersecurity, for instance, an attacker might alter malware data to trick the AI into labeling it safe.

Poisoning Attacks: These are highly sophisticated attacks. They focus on corrupting the training data used to build AI models by injecting harmful data into the training phase. This way, attackers can skew the AI's learning process, making it less reliable with time. Poisoning attacks can be a real pain to detect and have long-lasting negative impacts because they embed errors directly into the AI's foundational knowledge.

Transfer Attacks: Transfer attacks exploit the similarities between different AI models. Here, attackers develop adversarial examples for one AI system and then apply them to similar systems, effectively "transferring" the attack. The rationale is that since many AI systems share similar architectures, vulnerabilities in one can often be exploited in another to increase the risk of widespread harm.

Defense Mechanisms Against Adversarial AI

As adversarial AI threats grow, researchers and cybersecurity experts continually work on defense mechanisms to safeguard AI systems. This is an integral part of cyber security as a field of endeavor. Sadly, defending against adversarial AI is complex due to the constantly evolving nature of these attacks.

Adversarial Training: A promising method is adversarial training. This proactive measure exposes AI models to adversarial examples during their learning phase. By training on these deceptive inputs, models become better at recognizing and resisting similar attempts in the future. This approach can help build resilience against attacks attempting to exploit subtle data changes.

Defensive Distillation: Defensive distillation works by training a secondary AI model to act as a filter or shield for the primary system. The secondary model is designed to detect and reject adversarial inputs, creating an added layer of defense—like having a backup. Although experimental, defensive distillation has shown promise in fortifying AI systems against adversarial threats.

Improving Model Architecture: Strengthening the internal structure of AI models is another way to make it harder for adversarial attacks to succeed. By incorporating multiple validation layers or adding external verification checks, developers can build AI systems that are less sensitive to small data alterations, further fortifying them against adversarial examples.

Continuous Monitoring and Testing: Considering the adaptive nature of adversarial attacks, it is necessary to remain vigilant. Companies can fish out certain weaknesses by consistently testing AI models using different adversarial examples before the attackers do. Besides, real-time monitoring of AI behavior equally allows for the early detection of suspicious activities, enabling a quick response to potential threats.

Adversarial AI: A Growing Challenge

Believe it or not, adversarial AI is a rising challenge that threatens the security and reliability of AI systems across industries. Unlike traditional cyberattacks that target software flaws, adversarial AI manipulates the AI's learning process. This makes it harder for the AI to defend itself against such attacks. It's like taking someone down from the inside. Essentially, the more AI becomes increasingly critical to societal infrastructure, the more pressing the need for robust defenses against adversarial attacks becomes.

Furthermore, researchers, developers, and security experts are working together to counter these threats. Combining advanced model architectures, adversarial training, and ongoing research shows how much the field of AI security continues to evolve. This is the only way to keep up with these attackers. As AI continues to integrate into critical systems, effective defenses against adversarial attacks will be essential for maintaining trust and security.

CHAPTER FOUR

AI Vulnerabilities: When AI Becomes the Target

AI poisoning attacks are emerging threats, and security leaders at NIST and other industry leaders are warning that threat actors now employ this approach to test the resilience of security programs by manipulating the data being fed into the organization's AI systems.

From my experience working with several clients, I have seen poisoning attacks cause devasting effects, such as compromised model performance, security breaches, and faulty decision-making in critical systems such as autonomous driving, financial services, and healthcare. This chapter will explore poisoning attacks as a concept, discuss how they occur, and analyze some case studies to show their imminent risks to security systems.

Understanding AI Poisoning Attacks

At its core, an AI poisoning attack attempts to reengineer a machine learning model's learning process by feeding its training dataset with malicious or misleading data. Machine learning models depend heavily on vast amounts of data to make accurate decisions. However, if the integrity of this data is compromised, the model may learn incorrect patterns, which can lead to harmful or unbiased outcomes.

While traditional cybersecurity attacks often exploit system vulnerabilities or software weaknesses, poisoning attacks target datasets deployed in training AI models. This unique attack vector or method presents a significant challenge as the AI model, which functions in a black-box manner, is not directly attacked. Instead, the poisoning occurs during the training phase, which is the greatest vulnerability point of the model.

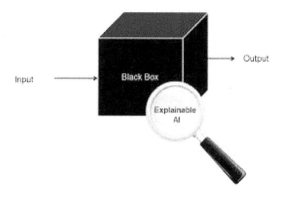

AI poisoning attacks are challenging to detect. Human operators may not detect slight changes made to the training data, but these changes can significantly affect the model's behavior in the long term.

Now, let's examine how the poisoning attacks work:

How AI Models Can Be Poisoned During Training

The training data is divided into two categories: labeled and unlabeled. Labeled data is crucial in supervised learning as it offers the model the correct outputs based on the input data. This allows the model to learn what outputs to expect from specific inputs.

By altering the input-output relationships, attackers can trick the models into learning incorrect associations. These attacks can manifest in different ways, depending on the objectives of the attackers and the type of AI system being targeted. Here are some of the most common methods of poisoning AI models:

Label Poisoning (Backdoor Poisoning)

Label or backdoor poisoning involves injecting mislabeled data into the training dataset. This subtle approach of altering the labels of specific data points can inject malicious instances that alter the behavior of the AI system during interference. For example, an attacker might inject a small percentage of images into a facial recognition training set mislabeled as "authorized" users. As a result, the model could learn to misclassify unauthorized individuals as authorized, creating a dangerous security loophole.

Training Data Poisoning

In this technique, the threat actor modifies a significant portion of the training data to skew the model's learning pathway toward a specific, often malicious, outcome. Let's assume the training data of an AI system that classifies emails as spam or non-spam has been injected with deceptive data, such as labeling some spam emails as legitimate. This could lead to the model classifying future spam emails, potentially allowing dangerous content to bypass spam filters. As I stated earlier, training data poisoning can cause long-term behavioral changes in the AI model and may be challenging to reverse. The more data the model processes, the more these incorrect patterns become entrenched in the system.

Model Inversion Attacks

Model inversion attacks involve exploiting the AI model's responses to infer sensitive information about the data it was trained on. An attacker carefully manipulates queries to the model and analyzes the output to extract confidential information about the training dataset. In other cases, threat actors can reconstruct parts of the original dataset by reverse-engineering the model's behavior. This attack raises significant privacy concerns, especially when the model has been trained on proprietary or sensitive information.

Stealth Attacks

Stealth attacks involve the strategic manipulation of training data that creates vulnerabilities in the model. Infiltration can remain undetected throughout the testing and development phases. The attacker injects subtle modifications to the data that are not obvious during model validation, but these changes introduce exploitative weaknesses when the model is deployed in real-world scenarios. For instance, in a healthcare application, a stealth poisoning attack could introduce minor changes to medical diagnosis data, leading to incorrect or dangerous diagnoses for specific patient demographics.

Stealth attacks target specific use cases or conditions, which means they may only manifest under that given scenario. This adds another layer of complexity to the defense against these variants.

Data Poisoning in Autonomous Vehicles.

Since 1984, when Carnegie Mellon University's Navlab Group pioneered research in autonomous vehicles (AVs), the field has gained increasing interest and become a major area in vehicular technology research. AVs integrate cutting-edge technologies such as AI and Big Data to ease traffic congestion and improve road safety. Autonomous vehicles depend heavily on AI models for critical decision-making, including object recognition, navigation, and environment awareness.

The accuracy and reliability of these systems are germane to ensuring the safety of passengers and pedestrians. However, the training datasets deployed to teach these models are vulnerable to poisoning attacks.

For instance, threat actors can subtly alter the images of traffic signs to deceive the object recognition model used by the AV. The manipulated images can be inserted into the model's training data, which can cause the vehicle to misclassify stop signs as speed limit signs.

This has grave consequences, as this misclassification can lead to fatal accidents. Human eyes cannot perceive the disruption on the stop sign, but it was enough to confuse the AI system. Therefore, we need defensive mechanisms to detect and mitigate such subtle attacks.

Healthcare AI systems

AI adoption in the healthcare industry is breathtaking. In its Q1 2024 survey of over 70 percent of respondents covering healthcare services and technology groups, payers, and providers, McKinsey revealed that they have already implemented or are about to implement Generative AI capabilities.

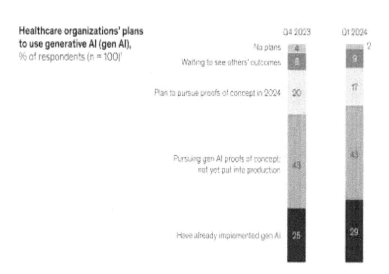

However, the sensitive nature of AI systems for medical diagnosis makes them prime targets for poisoning attacks. Let's explore a case study of how an AI system diagnoses diabetic retinopathy, which can lead to blindness if not properly managed or treated.

In this case, when mislabeled images were injected into the dataset, the attacker could cause the model to incorrectly diagnose healthy patients as having diabetic retinopathy and vice versa. Incorrect diagnoses put patients in both categories at risk of receiving or not receiving required treatments when they were needed.

The impact of a poisoning attack in healthcare can erode trust in AI systems and compromise patient safety. Thus, the security of the training data set has to be paramount for stakeholders.

Data Poisoning in Financial Fraud Detection

Financial institutions depend on AI models to analyze fraud transaction patterns and identify fraudulent activity. However, poisoning attacks on AI models can also have damaging consequences. Let's look at a scenario where a financial house's AI model for detecting credit card fraud was poisoned. The attacker can manipulate the training data by introducing fraudulent transactions labeled as legitimate. Consequently, the AI model learns to misclassify transactions and permits them to pass without getting noticed. There are twofold effects: the financial house will incur significant losses caused by undetected fraud, but legitimate transactions have also been flagged as fraudulent, disrupting customer service.

Defense Mechanisms Against Poisoning Attacks

While poisoning attacks are serious threats to AI models, researchers and companies can adopt the following defense mechanisms to mitigate risks.

Adversarial Training

An AI model can be exposed to adversarial examples during the training process. Training the model to detect and resist malicious scripts can make it resilient and resist malicious injection. This technique forces the model to learn from both clean and poisoned data, making it difficult for threat actors to manipulate.

Data Sanitization

It is imperative to clean and verify the integrity of the training data before deploying it to teach the AI model. The process of sanitization can include checking for anomalies, mislabeled data, or malicious inputs that could undermine the model's performance. Implementing strict data validation procedures will ensure that only clean and reliable data is used during training.

Differential Privacy

Differential Privacy techniques can be used to prevent model inversion attacks. Noise can be added to the data during the training process. This method ensures that attackers cannot extract or re-engineer individual data points, making it harder for adversaries to change the data or guess sensitive information.

Now, let's dive deeply into Model Evasion Attacks.

Model Evasion Attacks: Exploiting Weaknesses in AI Algorithms

As AI continues to be integrated into various industries, from finance to healthcare, it becomes imperative to begin to understand its vulnerabilities. A significant threat to deployed AI systems is called—model evasion attacks. It's, just as the name implies, sheer stealth operations. The goal is for these attacks to go undetected. In these attacks, the perpetrators manipulate inputs to cause the AI system to make wrong classifications without triggering alarms or drawing any attention. This is quite unlike poisoning attacks launched during the training phase. Model evasion attacks are way beyond the training phase of AI and target models that are already live and already in use in real-world applications. Now that we've gone through the basics, let's reach out for more details about this type of attack.

Understanding Model Evasion Attacks

Model evasion attacks are a type of adversarial attack where attackers have little or no interest in the training phase of the AI. They cause harm by altering the input data to deceive the AI model, leading to gross misclassifications. This tactic is particularly distressing as the attack happens after the model is deployed, as in when it is actively in use where it can cause more harm. For example, an AI system to detect fraudulent transactions could be tricked into labeling a fraudulent transaction as legitimate. This is achieved by making little, almost invisible changes to a few transaction details. These adjustments are usually subtle enough that humans can't easily detect them, but they are sufficient to mislead the AI model.

According to the European Union Agency for Cybersecurity, model evasion attacks comprise roughly 45% of adversarial attacks on deployed AI systems, usually in finance and cybersecurity. These attacks show how vulnerable these AI models can be irrespective of their seeming super abilities. It's obvious how attackers exploit any weaknesses within AI algorithms in search of ways to manipulate inputs to bypass the system's detection mechanisms.

How Attackers Exploit Weak Points in AI Algorithms

It's no secret that attackers use several techniques to exploit vulnerabilities in AI models. They manipulate inputs to trick the AI into making wrong decisions. In this section, we will take a closer look at some of the methods these attackers use:

1. Adversarial Examples

Firstly, we meet Adversarial examples again. They are carefully designed inputs that lead an AI model to make mistakes. If we take image recognition, for example, attackers might make slight changes to a photograph, like adjusting a few imperceptible pixels to the human eye, yet sufficient to confuse the AI model. A famous

2015 study by researchers Goodfellow, Shlens, and Szegedy showed that altering pixels in an image of a panda led the AI model to misclassify it as a gibbon. Although it seems insignificant, the effects are huge. This technique can be used in various situations, from fooling surveillance systems to evading fraud detection.

2. Gradient-Based Attacks

Gradient-based attacks lean more toward sabotaging the AI model's learning process. However, it's a bit more technical and more calculated. The attackers start by figuring out how different parts of an input influence the AI's decisions. This way, they can identify what aspects of the data to change to achieve a specific (usually incorrect) output. This approach is especially effective in deep learning models that depend heavily on gradient calculations to adjust their weights and improve accuracy. Research shows that gradient-based attacks can increase misclassification rates by 35% in high-stakes sectors like finance and cybersecurity. These attacks focus on deep learning algorithms by using minimal changes to trick the AI into making wrong predictions.

3. Transferability of Adversarial Attacks

One of the trickiest aspects of evasion attacks is something called transferability. This is where an adversarial example crafted specially to fool one AI model can also fool other similar models. In actuality, this gives attackers a huge advantage. Consider the classic killing two birds with one stone. Additionally, even if they don't have direct access to a particular AI model, they might still be able to bypass its defenses by working with a different, similar model. It's more like what works for one works for the other.

If we take fraud detection as a classic example, here's what could happen. The attackers could train their model on a dataset that's close enough to the one used by the target system. From there, they develop techniques to bypass their model's defenses, knowing full well that it will likely work on the target AI through transferability. Like it or not, transferability poses a serious problem in AI security, especially since adversarial strategies are constantly evolving. Studies show that transferability rates in these attacks can be as high as 80%, especially among models with similar architectures.

4. Exploiting Feature Blind Spots

We have already established that AI models depend on certain features in data to make their predictions. However, like those who design them, they have "blind spots." These blind spots are areas where AI accuracy falters, making them less reliable. The attackers can now leverage these weak points by crafting inputs designed to confuse the model, leading to more incorrect results.

For example, attackers might play with lighting or adjust subtle facial details to fool the AI in a facial recognition system, causing it to misidentify individuals. By zooming in on these specific vulnerabilities, attackers can sneak past detection, especially concerning high-stakes applications like security checks and identity verification.

Vulnerabilities in AI Models

Among other human abilities, AI models are designed to imitate, but they can have weak points, too. These weak points are loose ends that make them vulnerable to attacks. Usually, these vulnerabilities can vary depending on the model's structure and purpose. As a result, some types of models are at more risk than others. Especially unsupervised learning models, which learn from unlabeled data. Since these models do not have clear examples of what's correct or incorrect, they are easier for attackers to manipulate.

Below are a few key vulnerabilities that attackers commonly exploit.

1. Weak Generalization in Unsupervised Learning Models

Unsupervised learning models are replete with raw, unlabeled data. As a result, these models find patterns among the unlabeled data, making them useful for tasks like grouping similar data points or spotting strange patterns. However, these models can easily make mistakes since they are not trained with clear examples of correct answers. For instance, researchers have discovered that fraud detection models using unsupervised learning can be bypassed by making small changes to transaction details. So, by adjusting details to fall within the model's "normal" range, attackers can evade detection without setting off any alarms.

2. Overfitting to Specific Features

Overfitting occurs when an AI model depends too much on certain features in its training data. As a result of this uncanny dependence, they become less effective when dealing with new data. This way, attackers can take advantage by creating inputs different enough from what the model has learned to deceive it. For example, attackers might slightly modify some parts of a malicious code in detecting malware, causing the AI to classify it as safe wrongly. A 2023 report by IBM showed that over 60% of AI models used in malware detection were vulnerable to evasion attacks because of overfitting. This shows how important models that can easily and flexibly adapt to new data are.

3. Lack of Robustness in High-Dimensional Data

Many AI models, particularly deep learning ones, deal with high-dimensional data. The thing with high-dimensional data is the numerous variables involved. Also, these complex data spaces often deal with intricate boundaries between different categories. This means that even the smallest changes to input data can cause the model to be misclassified. For instance, in finance, fraud detection models analyze a wide range of transaction features, so the slightest adjustments to just a few can allow fraudulent transactions to go unnoticed. A 2022 study shows that about 40% of high-dimensional AI models in finance are prone to errors due to small input changes.

Case Study: Evasion Attacks in Practice

Evasion attacks differ from what we wish for, as they can disrupt various AI applications. The list is gradually growing, from cybersecurity to facial recognition. Below are some examples demonstrating how these attacks work and their potential risks.

Case Study: Evasion Attacks in Malware Detection

We can see an excellent example of evasion attacks in cybersecurity, especially malware detection. Many security systems depend on AI to scan files to ensure they are free from malicious attempts. Most cyber attackers only need to change the malware code slightly to remain undetected. When attackers succeed in changing nonessential parts of the code or file structure, they can deceive the AI model into grouping the malware as safe.

In a certain situation, researchers used a gradient-based technique to make small changes to the binary features of malware. This made the AI misidentify them as utterly harmless. The malware was able to bypass the security system without getting detected. This shows a need for more solid defenses against this cybersecurity problem.

Case Study: Evasion Attacks on Facial Recognition Systems

Suppose an unauthorized personnel enters a high-security area, bypassing security cameras and surveillance systems. That seems a little ghostly. In this case, the unauthorized personnel isn't a ghost but a regular person using evasion attacks on facial recognition systems. Usually, they wear innocent glasses designed specially to disrupt AI-powered facial recognition systems. This disruption is smoothly executed without triggering any alarms. The AI is deceived into identifying the intruder as an authorized personnel member and immediately granting access.

Researchers in a recent study have demonstrated how easily these facial recognition systems are misled with tiny adjustments to the code. This means that AI-powered facial recognition systems used in exclusive environments may not be as secure as we thought. Therefore, there is an increased need to continually improve these high-tech systems, keeping them one step ahead of cybercriminals.

Defense Strategies Against Evasion Attacks

Equipping the defense strategies used to protect AI models is of utmost importance since evasion attacks continue to become more sophisticated. Let us consider some of the top strategies, including how they assist AI in resisting these attacks for a more secure society.

1. Adversarial Training

Adversarial training is the defense that exposes the AI model to tricky, manipulated examples, just as in poisoning attacks. The kinds used by attackers enable AI to develop and build innate resistance against them. It's like building an immune system against invaders.

Research carried out by Goodfellow and colleagues showed how adversarial training can reduce an AI model's vulnerability by about 50%. Essentially, models trained with this method become experts at identifying and recognizing these deceptive techniques, making them more resilient to attacks in the real world.

2. Regularization Techniques

Regularization is all about creating a more generalized learning system for AI. This way, they can become more independent of a narrow information set, as with overfitting. This allows for flexibility in unfamiliar situations like cyberattacks. An excellent example is the L2 regularization and dropout methods. According to a study at MIT, regularized models handled complex datasets against evasion attacks 30% times better than their unregularized counterparts. This type of intervention aims to equip the model with a broader understanding so that it is less susceptible to tiny adjustments evident in evasion attacks.

3. Ensemble Models

Ensemble models, as the name implies, are all about togetherness. They pool strengths to tackle a common enemy. The key here is combining the predictions of several models instead of relying on only one. This makes it more difficult for one manipulated input to deceive the AI system.

One easy way to exemplify this is to imagine a cybersecurity need to analyze network traffic. Here, an ensemble of AI models can be set up where one picks up suspicious patterns that others might overlook. An IBM 2023 study found that ensemble models quickly detected malware to reduce evasion rates by over 40%. In other words, there is a need for more teamwork, even among AI. It's a foolproof way to build lasting cybersecurity.

4. Robust Feature Extraction

Think of robust feature extraction, like training to recognize a face, strictly by the permanent features that can't be easily altered. In facial recognition technology, these unchanging stable features include but are not limited to stable facial structures such as eye and nose position. This directly contrasts with quickly changing details such as lightning, background, etc. This method of focusing on more permanent features makes it more challenging for attackers to mislead the AI.

We indeed need to continue improving our defenses against cyber attacks. However, protecting AI involves more than mere technology. Big questions arise about privacy, fairness, and who bears the brunt when things go wrong. Chapter 5 will discuss the rules and ethical choices surrounding AI's role in cybersecurity and how to keep innovation and people safe.

CHAPTER FIVE

Building AI-Resilient Cybersecurity Strategies

As we have seen in previous chapters, the ever-evolving cyber threat has rendered traditional perimeter-based models inadequate in keeping networks secure. The advantage of Zero Trust architecture is its stringent trust policy, especially regarding network security, be it user, application, or device, and it doesn't matter whether they're within or outside your network. Under Zero Trust, you must remember that every access request needs to be explicitly verified, treated as if a potential breach lurks in the background, and allowed the least-privilege access- the three core principles of zero trust architecture. While these principles can significantly help to boost your security, bringing an AI into the mix can make these even more effective. An AI's real-time capabilities in your zero trust can allow you to create a cybersecurity framework that is robust and effectively responsive to sophisticated, dynamic threats.

Integrating AI into your zero trust gives your cybersecurity network real-time monitoring and adaptive capabilities, significantly boosting your zero-trust effectiveness and efficiency. That's because AI can process massive amounts of data at an incredibly high speed, allowing it to identify patterns and possible anomalies that could go unnoticed in a traditional cybersecurity protocol. AI, as you must have known, can effectively monitor user behavior patterns, identify any deviation from the norms, and, if found, red flags them as a potential threat before they can make their way throughout the system. For example, an employee who previously logs in front of a particular location now wants to access the network from a different location at a questionable hour; the AI's ability to analyze this sudden behavior could help to ensure that such anomalies do not go unnoticed instantly.

As the AI learns continuously from data, it dynamically adjusts and enhances your security policies without requiring manual adjustments. These capabilities give the AI a rich adaptability that perfectly aligns with your need for zero trust regarding least privilege access and constant verification.

A core principle in zero trust requires minimal access for every user. However, implementing this across a larger organization with diverse needs can be challenging. Again, AI plays a critical role here by allowing for adaptive authentication while dynamically adjusting security measures according to the risk profile for each access request.

An adaptive posture of AI creates an ideal balance by strengthening security in a high-risk situation and streamlining processes at low-risk times, which brings about a seamless experience for the user. If you log in from a recognized device at a secure location, AI can quickly recognize the low risk and grant access. However, if an unrecognized device from a new or different location accesses the network, the AI could prompt additional security measures, such as multi-factor authentication, to ensure that all access attempts are legitimate. Such adaptability brought about by AI can make larger organizations' zero trust less cumbersome while ensuring maximum security at places that matter most.

The automated policy creation and management AI can help reinforce your zero trust principles. An issue faced within a large-scale and dynamic network is that policies can quickly become redundant as new technologies and associated threats emerge. So, instead of relying on static rules and policies, AI can step in by helping you to continuously update your policies based on real-time insights and the changing threat landscapes. For example, suppose a phishing attack threatens a particular region. In that case, AI can automatically tighten access control for that region, making it harder for malicious attackers to exploit existing vulnerabilities. These adaptive adjustments reduce the need for manual policy updates and can make your zero trust more responsive to evolving threats. Therefore, AI can support a dynamic and agile security environment, responding appropriately to evolving threats by proactively refining security rules.

The AI's behavioral analytics is yet another area that can strengthen your zero trust. The assumed breach principle in your zero trust means that unusual activity, whether internal or external, could be a sign of threat. So, AI can analyze the behavior of each user and device within the network and create a profile for each based on a regular pattern. Assuming you originally explicitly accessed it during office hours and somehow begin downloading sensitive data at night hours, the AI can immediately flag this behavior or charge it as suspicious. This analytical behavior is beyond what is obtainable in a traditional system, and the insight gained from these behavioral analytics gives an added layer of security by ensuring that abnormal activities are identified quickly and timely enough while protecting critical data assets from internal and external breaches.

The AI's ability to facilitate real-time threat intelligence can further boost your zero trust. More than just identifying internal anomalies, as you must know, an AI can equally analyze external data from various sources, keeping your systems updated on trends and emerging risks. For example, if a certain malware is trending, an AI can proactively adjust security policies to prevent that threat from spreading across the network. It helps reinforce the' assumed breach principle' by preparing for potential attacks before they appear. Such a proactive approach would make your zero trust architecture more effective and shift your organization's protective cybersecurity posture from reactive to being prevented. It also allows you the appropriate time to deal with potential threats before they get hold of your system to compromise it.

While integrating AI into your zero trust can come with many benefits, you may need some help with implementation, such as managing false positives and ensuring scalability. Still, AI can excel in helping you manage false positives by learning what makes up normal behavior over time to make more correct decisions and reduce unnecessary alerts. Such a level of accuracy allows your cybersecurity team to concentrate resources on genuine threats instead of wasting time on false alerts, which can make your zero-trust implementation less resource-intensive. AI can also help your zero trust policy scale effortlessly while bringing onboard new devices, users, and applications without requiring extensive manual adjustments. AI eases the burden of managing access policies by automation, which helps you maintain a secure environment as your organization's responsibilities expand.

So, to implement an AI-enhanced zero trust, you must first apply it to high-value assets like critical systems and sensitive data assets. After implementing AI-driven security measures, you can extend them gradually to other parts of your network to incorporate adaptive authentication and automate policy management. As the AI continuously gathers and analyses data, it will improve its accuracy and provide you with feedback that can help refine your zero-trust policies. All these processes strengthen your organization's security and optimize it continuously to be responsive to new challenges.

AI-Driven Continuous Authentication and Monitoring

The ever-presence of sophisticated cyber threats makes maintaining a higher vigilance necessary. Traditional cybersecurity authentication measures such as multi-factor authentication passwords and usernames come with their data and systems security limitations. For as long as a user gains an entry after an authentication, they can enjoy extended access, creating vulnerabilities, especially if a hacker gains access. However, with AI-driven continuous authentication and monitoring, you can find a solution that creates a more dynamic and responsive security framework that adapts in real time. Instead of a user having a one-time verification process, the AI would prompt them to authenticate and verify through their session continuously, thus adding a critical layer to your cybersecurity where every access point and action is checked and verified against potential threats.

The AI's real-time monitoring capabilities are crucial to achieving continuous authentication. AI allows your security systems to evaluate user behavior and their interactions in the system throughout their session. It analyzes user behavior patterns like typing speed, location, or mouse movements and establishes a baseline profile for individual users. Each time there is a deviation from the established baseline profile, the system can flag it as a potential threat, needing additional verification or restricting access automatically, and, as a result, strengthens your security with an additional layer of scrutiny in ways that traditional static authentication methods cannot match.

Also, AI-driven continuous authentication allows your systems to maintain greater flexibility while securing vital information. A system that can initially allow full user access based on their profile and monitor users' actions as the session progresses. Let's say the user went from their normal activities and started to access files, which are not a typical part of their workflow; AI would prompt additional automation steps such as restricting access or multi-factor authentication. This adaptive measure balances usability and security while providing users seamless access during a risk-prone event and enhancing protection against suspicious activities. Such adaptability can align with your organization's growing need for a security solution that would not disrupt its workflow but still allow robust protection against unauthorized access.

The dynamic posture of AI-driven monitoring can help your organization stay ahead of the evolving threat landscape. As you must know, the ever-evolving cyber threats and the changing nature of attacks are increasingly becoming adept at bypassing static security arrangements. But with AI-driven continuous monitoring and adaptability, your systems can rapidly respond to new and emerging cyber threats. The AI capabilities to draw from vast datasets and constantly update threat feeds to keep up with the latest pattern behavior in hacking techniques give your organization a proactive approach to detecting and mitigating threats before they escalate, reducing any chances of a successful attack.

Still, AI-driven monitoring can enhance your organization's security resilience by reducing false positives, a common issue in the traditional monitoring architecture. Having a high volume of false positives can tire your security team and reduce their efficiency in detecting real threats due to alert fatigue. But

AI refines its understanding of what should or shouldn't constitute normal behavior for an individual user and system over time, and thanks to its learning process, allows it to tell a legitimate variation in user behavior for each user from an actual security threat.

Continuous authentication and monitoring are especially advantageous when mobile access or remote work is prevalent. Maintaining security becomes more complex as more employees work remotely or use different devices to access the corporate network. However, AI's ability to continuously monitor sessions in real-time, irrespective of their locations, becomes vital because it ensures that security is consistent across locations and devices even when users switch from a mobile phone to a PC or entirely sign in from a different network.

AI-driven continuous authentication thrives in improving cybersecurity and helping stream-stream user experience. Imagine a traditional cybersecurity measure that frequently requires login details or multiple authentications; wouldn't that be disruptive, especially for your employees who may need quick access to resources? By establishing baseline behavior patterns with continuous monitoring in the background, AI can significantly reduce the need for constant and intrusive authentications, allowing users to enjoy seamless sessions with systems that require additional verification only when it detects suspicious behavior.

Therefore, integrating AI into your continuous authentication and monitoring can bring long-term adaptability and scalability. So, as your organization grows, its security needs grow, too, because more devices, users, and access points will come on board. With the AI's ability to learn and adapt its functions, your organization can scale as it helps you adjust to the increasing complexities of monitoring more extensive networks. So, you can use AI-driven solutions to configure your organization's evolution, which adds new behavioral models as necessary while adapting to the dynamics in user behavior over time. Such scalability makes your cybersecurity more robust without requiring frequent manual adjustments or elaborate reconfiguration, making it cost-effective.

AI-Enhanced Threat Intelligence

What comes to your mind when you hear AI-enhanced threat intelligence? It is a form of intelligence that leverages artificial intelligence to gather, analyze, and interpret massive amounts of data. Cybersecurity data in real-time allows one to gain a deeper insight into potential threats. It is a proactive move in threat detection, unlike the reactive approach in traditional means. AI's proactive approach is its ability to sift through vast datasets quicker and more accurately than any human analyst can.

AI-enhanced intelligence learns threat patterns from new data, which allows AI adaptability to emerging threat tactics used by cybercriminals. Such adaptability empowers your system to detect previously unknown threat patterns, reducing the risk of any surprise attack incident. AI-driven threat intelligence can provide real-time and adaptive layers to your cybersecurity defense, enhancing your organization's ability to anticipate and mitigate threats before they spread out, giving it a strategic advantage in navigating the current dynamic threat landscape.

Leveraging AI for threat intelligence collection and analysis has become a vital part of our system's cybersecurity resilience today. The sheer volume of data usually faced by cyber teams, like those from network logs to alerts managed in traditional cybersecurity settings, can be overwhelming and even delay adequate response time to emerging threats. However, AI can relieve these human analysts of their burden by changing these processes and enabling systems to gather and analyze massive amounts of threat data automatically, at great speed and efficiency.

The value of AI in enhancing threat intelligence begins with its capacity to access a wide range of data sources at once. Threat intelligence can be gathered from anywhere, whether internal sources like user behavior, application logs, and network traffic or external sources such as social media, the dark web, and open-source intelligence. So, AI-driven tools can gather data from all these sources by continuously collecting them into a comprehensive framework of the threat landscape that human analysts would initially need help to piece together manually.

While data is collected, AI's analytical tools begin the interpretation process immediately. The machine learning algorithms allow AI to identify patterns and anomalies present in a stream of data, signaling potential risks or suspicious activity. Fortunately, these algorithms extend beyond the traditional rule-based detection approach; instead, they learn from past patterns and use that knowledge to recognize new patterns of threats. This approach improves the accuracy in detecting threats and minimizes the number of false positives. The AI's capabilities in predictive analytics are quite transformative; with this predictive model, the AI can anticipate potential future risks and attack vectors according to observed behavior, which adds an extra layer to your pre-emptive security.

AI's intelligent contributions are intrinsic to an automated response mechanism. After identifying a threat, the AI system prioritizes based on the identified risk level and then initiates a predefined response action by isolating a compromised system, blocking out a suspicious IP address, or alerting the relevant persons in charge.

Also, AI can enhance your threat intelligence by enabling real-time collaboration across your organization. The AI's ability to aggregate threat intelligence from different entities creates a collaborative defence framework that benefits the network. Therefore, sharing anonymized threat data across industries would help organizations identify and respond to global threats more effectively. For instance, an organization encounters a novel cyberattack technique. AI systems can quickly analyze this intelligence and disseminate it across the various organizations within the network, serving them with early warning of potential risks. Such a model of collaborative efforts leverages the collective power of AI to develop a network of shared defenses where proactive countermeasures are used to combat threats immediately after being identified.

However, leveraging AI for your threat intelligence would require careful planning and implementation to limit potential bottlenecks. A primary challenge here is the extent of data quality and integrity. As you know, AI depends on extensive data, and if information is incomplete and biased, then the AI's predictability and supposed actions may become unreliable. So, to avoid this, it is essential to use data from high-quality sources and constantly monitor the output of the AI for accuracy.

Again, there is another challenge, and it is one in real-time. While building a reliable AI-powered threat intelligence network depends on proactive cybersecurity measures like real-time monitoring and threat management, it comes with considerable challenges. These include data quality, integration complexities, evolving attack techniques, and scalability. A good understanding of these issues and satisfactorily addressing them is essential in helping you develop that resilient AI-powered threat intelligence network.

One common challenge in real-time threat intelligence is the sheer volume of data to be simultaneously processed. As previously noted,

AI requires a vast amount of accurate data to function effectively. Collecting massive amounts of internal and external data comes with challenges. First, each data source may have a distinct format and structure, complicating their integration into a single and cohesive threat intelligence platform.

Another critical challenge is scalability. We can all agree that the volume and diversity of data points to be monitored and secured expands as your network and organization grow. An AI-powered threat intelligence system can help you scale seamlessly to accommodate new data streams without compromising accuracy and speed. However, this scalability can become more complex in a real-time environment where there happens to be a delay, as there could be a missed threat. So integrating an AI model that is adaptable to your expanding infrastructure without sacrificing performance can be a delicate task, especially as it has to do with balancing storage and processing power with the need for an immediate and top-notch threat analysis.

Also, a dynamic challenge can come from cybersecurity threats' continuous and adaptive nature as more cyber-attackers leverage advanced tools to manipulate AI-driven threat intelligence systems. For example, an adversary can use adversarial attacks to deceive AI algorithms by embedding tiny signals within data patterns to exploit the reliance on AI pattern recognition. These tactics can deceive systems into generating inaccurate assessments or looking past specific threats.

Compliance and privacy issues can also arise as your organization tries to integrate external threat intelligence into its real-time AI systems. While sharing intelligence across networks can provide holistic resilience, it should comply with data protection regulations and privacy laws like the GDPR. Therefore, your organization must develop a framework that facilitates secure anonymized data sharing to benefit from collective intelligence without countering data privacy regulations.

Now, look into cybersecurity domains transformed by AI and machine learning. AI and machine learning (ML) are transforming various domains in cybersecurity, which can enhance your organization's capabilities to identify, respond to, and even prevent threats in ways that were initially impossible to do. Through automation processes, learning from a vast pool of data, and adapting to emerging threats, AI and ML have reshaped. They are still reshaping cybersecurity functions, from threat detection and network security to data loss prevention and identity verification.

Threat detection is a critical domain in cybersecurity, where AI and ML have improved significantly. Traditional cybersecurity systems mainly rely on predefined rules and established threat signatures, making it challenging to detect novel cyberattacks under this system. However, AI excels in recognizing patterns and identifying anomalies that may point to a potential threat. AI-driven systems can flag deviations that could go unnoticed under traditional systems, even when they involve previously unknown attack methods, by analyzing real-time network traffic, system logs, and user behavior.

Also, AI is championing advancements in network security by enhancing cybersecurity systems' ability to monitor, analyze, and effectively respond to intrusions. Machine learning algorithms, on the other hand, can analyze traffic flow across a complex network to identify any unusual behavior or patterns that could indicate an intrusion. Together, these systems can identify abnormal data flow, detect port scanning, and pick up on unusual activity that could indicate a potential breach. Yet AI enables a comprehensive approach to detecting and preventing potential cyberattacks. This automated network analysis allows organizations to effectively protect systems even in massive data volumes and complex data structures.

Identity verification and access control are other domains where AI and ML bring about tremendous improvements. You should know by now how traditional cybersecurity access control methods like rule-based permission and passwords are increasingly vulnerable to social engineering attacks and breaches. But with AI-powered systems, you can integrate biometric data, contextual factors such as device and location data, and even behavioral analysis to verify identity more accurately. ML algorithms can learn from previous users' behaviors and use them to detect and flag potential compromises like an abnormal usage pattern or unusual login location.

AI and ML are making strides in malware detection, too. While conventional antivirus software requires known signatures to identify malware, making it ineffective against new threats, an AI model trained on a vast dataset of malware behavior and signatures can identify malware based on its behavioral patterns even if such malware has been altered or has no known signatures.

Data loss prevention (DLP) is another domain that has benefited significantly from AI. Protecting sensitive data requires continuous data flow monitoring, especially in organizations where information sharing occurs across several devices, networks, and applications. With AI DLP systems, data patterns can be analyzed and detected by monitoring where data is accessed, altered, or shared. The AI-powered systems then automatically flag or block the unauthorized transfer of any sensitive data or detect potential data leaks before they escalate into more significant security issues.

Collaboration Between Humans and AI

The collaboration between humans and AI in cybersecurity is essential in helping organizations achieve a balanced and resilient cybersecurity. While AI processes vast data, detects anomalies, and automates routine tasks, we need human expertise in interpreting, validating, and acting upon AI-driven oversights. This kind of partnership brings about a robust system where AI manages tedious, repetitive tasks such as monitoring network traffic for unusual patterns or identifying suspicious behavior in real time. Similarly, cybersecurity professionals can focus on more sophisticated tasks requiring human intuition, contextual understanding, and ethical considerations.

Humans and AI working together can strengthen each other's weaknesses. Human oversight is also crucial for refining AI algorithms, correcting false positives, and ensuring that AI effectively adapts to evolving threats. Through this arrangement, your organization can develop a cybersecurity framework that is agile, reliable, and ready to face challenges now and shortly.

The value of a human-AI hybrid security model lies in building a resilient and adaptive cybersecurity strategy that leverages the best of humans and AI. While AI can analyze vast amounts of data in real time, detect anomalies, and respond to potential threats at incredible speed, it cannot address cyber threats' nuanced and dynamic nature. You have to understand that cybersecurity is as much about intent and context as it is about data patterns, and humans can bring on board qualities such as critical thinking, ethical judgment, and contextual awareness. For example, AI can detect an anomaly in a network activity. Still, human analysts need to determine whether or not it is a threat or simply an average behavioral deviation from the established baseline.

Human intervention is a reliable go-to in situations that require critical decisions.

The human-AI model also enhances continuous learning and improvements. That's why cybersecurity analysts train AI algorithms to improve their recognition capabilities on emerging threats, and AI provides the analyst with insights about new patterns and vulnerabilities in return. Such a feedback loop system enables humans and their AI systems to improve operations and effectiveness while adapting to evolving cyber threats and galvanizing approaches according to new intelligence.

AI's tendency to produce false positives and alert on not-so-behavior due to pattern deviations can cause unnecessary alert fatigue if not correctly managed. Human intervention can help prioritize these alerts by discerning real threats from noise, making the overall security process more efficient and saving the team from the stress of too many unnecessary alerts.

This hybrid approach can also help build resilience against attacks that exploit the limitations of AIs, such as adversarial attacks that attempt to trick AI models. So, each time an AI algorithm comes across situations that they're not cut out for or programmed to handle, human expertise can step in the way to assess and put any potential risks under control while maintaining system integrity.

Now, let's delve into the use of human oversight to address AI limitations.

First, we must acknowledge that human oversight is significant when addressing the limitations, especially in a high-stakes cybersecurity landscape. Although AI can bring appreciable efficiency into threat detection, data analysis, and disaster recovery management, these capabilities have inherent limitations. Without human oversights, these limitations can spiral into vulnerabilities, including blind spots in threat detection, ethical concerns, and false positives. The involvement of humans allows AI to operate responsively, effectively, and by organizational security standards and values.

A fundamental limitation of AI in cybersecurity is that it depends on historical data and patterns. While AI algorithms are trained on past data to identify known threats accurately, they may struggle to identify novel or adaptive cyberattacks that deviate from established norms. Malicious attackers frequently develop new innovative ways to bypass AI's predictive ability, knowing that even though an AI may be fast, it still lacks creativity. However, human analysts can recognize contextual deviations and new tactics and adapt their strategies in dealing with emerging threats while receiving guidance from AI systems to refine their models accordingly—this way, the unknown unknowns effectively stem from slipping through AI's defenses.

Another limitation of AI is its high sensitivity to data quality. If there are inconsistencies, biases, or gaps in training data, it can have an effect that ripples throughout its performance. However, human oversight can ensure that the data used in training AI has not been poisoned. Also, cybersecurity teams can bring insights and judgment that AI alone can't provide, especially as it involves critical decisions like prioritizing how to interpret ambiguous findings. Human insights help minimize errors in AI decision-making, enhancing security and reducing the chances of expensive mistakes.

Additionally, human oversights can help counter AI's penchant for false positives. AI lacks the contextual awareness to tell the difference between a real threat and harmless anomalies, which can lead to an overwhelming number of alerts. However, humans play a balancing role here by reviewing flagged quarries, analyzing intents, and adjusting AI to improve accuracy.

We must end this by discussing ethical considerations; human oversight is crucial. AI lacks moral reasoning and a sense of accountability. Therefore, decisions made by AI, especially in sensitive domains such as data handling and privacy, can unintentionally breach legal requirements or ethical standards.

Human oversight is needed to provide the ethical and moral framework to ensure that AI-driven cybersecurity measures and the organization's ethics stay within privacy limits. Cybersecurity teams can monitor AI actions, ensure it complies with laws and ethical standards, and prevent AI misuse by setting boundaries that AI models cannot understand.

CHAPTER SIX

Future Threats and Challenges:
Looking Ahead

Quantum computing is making a great impact in the world of computers. It is poised to change all we know about cybersecurity protocols, particularly when discussing AI and cryptography. But what is quantum computing all about? It is a technology well suited to solving problems beyond what classical computers can do. Just like a double-edged sword for your cybersecurity, it doesn't only bring promising advancements. Still, it can also come along with new and formidable challenges, especially for AI-driven systems, which are today an integral part of modern cybersecurity infrastructures. It has the potential to not only compromise existing encryption but also to render existing cybersecurity methods vulnerable. Therefore, the intersection between AI and quantum computing is fast becoming one of the most pressing challenges in the future.

The more sophisticated quantum computing becomes, the more intense its impact on cybersecurity, particularly because it can expose traditional forms of encryption. Popular encryption methods in vogue today, such as Elliptic curve cryptography(ECC) and Rivest-Shamir-Adleman(RSA), use mathematical problems that are presently and computationally impossible for classical computers to handle and solve in a reasonable timeframe. But with quantum algorithms like Shor's algorithm, systems solve large numbers at incredible speed, threatening the security of any data you can imagine being encrypted under these methods. This could only mean one thing: AI-driven cybersecurity systems that rely on encryption and data privacy may become vulnerable to quantum-based attacks, a looming threat that calls for attention.

The good side of quantum computing is that it can enhance AI, especially in tasks like machine learning, cryptographic analysis, and optimization. Interestingly, the computational power of a quantum machine can significantly improve the speed of the number of times the AI model is trained, giving it the capability to process massive datasets and insights within seconds. Here is the not-so-good side now; adversaries can use this power and speed to train models faster than they ever could for their malicious intent, such as refining AI-bases cyberattacks or developing an advanced hacking technique.

But that is not the only not-so-good side of quantum computing. Grover's algorithm is yet another quantum algorithm that poses a potential threat to the cryptographic hash function by weakening it and cutting short the time needed for brute-force searches. As it is well known to cybersecurity experts, the functions are used extensively in cybersecurity to underpin anything from blockchain technology to password protection. So, Grover's algorithm could render an AI system that relies on hash-based cybersecurity protocols vulnerable to unprecedented attacks when cybercriminals use quantum computing to breach these protections faster than they could have ever done.

Therefore, AI and quantum computing can add an extra layer of complexity to our cybersecurity, and a future where quantum AI becomes accessible to both cybercriminals and cybersecurity experts can be a gamble in which the balance of power could swing dramatically to either side. So, while quantum computing can benefit defense security measures with its faster and more complex capabilities for data analysis, it can also be exploited by cybercriminals for offensive purposes like accelerated threat detection evasion and could even enhance the sophistication and stealthiness of cyberattacks. With such a dual potential possessed by quantum AI, cybersecurity strategies must evolve rapidly, considering the advancements in AI and quantum resistance measures for a more robust defense. The more reason cybersecurity teams and experts must be well prepared for these new forms of attacks that leverage the capabilities of quantum AI.

Next, let's look into preparation for the cybersecurity challenges of quantum AI.

Now, while anticipating threats due to quantum AI, you must remember that preparing your cybersecurity infrastructures to resist quantum and AI-driven attacks is essential, and the most important step is transitioning to quantum-resistant cryptography. The quantum-resistant algorithms are well designed to counter attacks from quantum computers, unlike the traditional cryptographic security methods, which can provide a layer of protection against the vulnerabilities brought about by advancements in quantum computing. Other proposed and viable quantum-resistant techniques are multivariate polynomial cryptography, code-base cryptography, and lattice-base cryptography. These post-quantum cryptographic methods will help your organization protect data assets and secure communications in a possible quantum AI world.

Also, AI can enhance your quantum-resistant strategies by helping your cybersecurity team identify potential vulnerabilities in real-time. Its ability to analyze massive datasets quicker allows AI to detect anomalies that may signal attempts to compromise your system's quantum-resistant encryption. With these real-time monitoring capabilities, cybersecurity teams can respond swiftly to any potential threats and, as a result, mitigate risks. Additionally, AI-driven cyber threat intelligence systems can continuously evolve in pattern recognition associated with quantum-based attacks and adapt their defenses as they become more common.

Additionally, AI-driven systems can enhance quantum threat resilience through automated responses to threats or cybersecurity breaches. For example, your cybersecurity team can train machine learning algorithms to identify quantum-based attack patterns and automatically initiate pre-defined countermeasures. Such automated responses allow your security systems to operate with almost zero human intervention, making countering these threats faster and more efficient. Suppose your organization should go ahead and integrate AI into its incident response system to make it faster and more efficient. In that case, it will be set up to address quantum-based threats proactively and counter them before they escalate.

Another vital aspect in your preparation for the cybersecurity challenges of quantum AI includes fostering interdisciplinary collaboration between cybersecurity professionals, AI experts, and quantum computing research. The cross-fertilization of information across these fields is necessary to foster the development of innovative solutions that can address the unique challenges of quantum AI. Therefore, the working together of experts from these fields can help test the resilience of existing security measures, develop new strategies tailored to the evolving threat landscape, and identify potential vulnerabilities earlier. With such a collaboration, organizations can advance quantum-resistant cryptography and enhance AI detection and response mechanisms, ultimately strengthening their cybersecurity ecosystem.

Preparing well enough for quantum AI's impact on cybersecurity also requires a shift in policy and regulatory frameworks. The governments and policymakers in places where our businesses operate must establish guidelines and standards to ensure that organizations are well protected against these threats by quantum. The standards may include mandates for conducting regular risk assessments, implementing AI-driven security, or adopting post-quantum cryptographic techniques and systems. When these measures are enforced, policymakers will promote a uniform level of protection across various organizations that can minimize the risk of quantum AI-driven cyber threats.

Education and awareness are also important in evolving cybersecurity strategies. That is, cybersecurity professionals need to stay updated on new advancements in AI and quantum computing if they must effectively counter these emerging threats. They can keep pace with the rapidly evolving quantum AI landscape by collaborating with friends in the field, attending conferences, and engaging in continuous learning. Such a proactive approach can allow your organization's cybersecurity team to adapt to potent cybersecurity strategies that are just right for your business while fortifying systems against future challenges.

It would be best to consider ethical concerns in your preparation, as it would also play a vital role in shaping your organization's development and deployment of quantum AI in cybersecurity. Quantum AI must be used responsibly to avoid abuses, just like any other powerful technology. Therefore, establishing ethical guidelines for quantum AI applications can help mitigate the risks of misuse or exploitative purposes. The guidelines should border on transparency, accountability, and data privacy to ensure that quantum is used in ways that compensate for cybersecurity efforts and do not go against societal values.

AI in Autonomous Systems and IoT Security

In a time like ours, when AI is integrated into everything from IoT(Internet of Things) to drones, it brings opportunities and serious challenges to our cybersecurity ecosystem. Although autonomous systems powered by AI and IoT smart infrastructure bring convenience, safety, and improved efficiency, inherent risks and vulnerabilities can still greatly impact everything about our lives, from personal privacy to national security.

AI-powered autonomous systems, such as robotic assistants, drones, and self-driving vehicles, are fast dominating the healthcare, defense, logistics, and transportation industries. All these systems rely heavily on machine learning algorithms for their task execution, navigating their environment, and making reliable decisions with little human intervention. While all these developments are good for us and our business, their increasing autonomy calls for a greater security concern that must not be overlooked. The concerns are:

Vulnerability to Cyber Attacks: A key concern about AI-controlled autonomous systems is their vulnerability, which can be exploited in cyberattacks. Autonomous vehicles and drones are always data hungry, and they continuously collect, analyze, and react to data in their environment, unlike traditional security systems. This is the ugly side; their constant data receiving makes them susceptible to potentially different cyberattacks like data poisoning, where data is maliciously fed into the AI system and manipulated by its decision-making algorithm. So if, let's say, an attacker gains control over an autonomous vehicle, the attacker can override its control and redirect it or even cause a system shutdown generally, which could lead to disastrous outcomes, particularly in the defense or transportation sector, as we saw in chapter two in this book.

This constant data flow makes them susceptible to various attacks, such as data poisoning, in which malicious data is fed to the AI system to manipulate its decision-making. If an attacker gains access to the control systems of an autonomous vehicle, they could potentially redirect it, override its controls, or shut down its systems altogether, leading to disastrous outcomes, especially in critical sectors like transportation or defense.

Privacy and Surveillance Issues: As you would have seen in many systems equipped with data gathering capabilities like high-tech sensors and cameras able to perceive their surroundings in detail. For example, a drone used in delivery service or surveillance can inadvertently collect private information from the public, which can significantly concern people's privacy. Well, if under the control of good guys, their actions can be regulated by established policies. But again, there is a risk that unauthorized parties could hack the data or intercept the algorithm responsible for AI's functions and gain control over it. So, suppose you happen to find yourself in this space as the good guy. In that case, you must weigh the privacy risks and implement the necessary privacy policies to protect people's privacy rights.

Decision-Making in High-Stakes Environments: You will encounter unique cybersecurity challenges if autonomous systems operate in complex and high-stakes environments, such as defense or healthcare. Let's say a medical delivery got infused with faulty sensor data and made a wrong decision; it might cause it to deliver life-saving medication at the wrong location or even end up crashing, leading to harm. In defense, autonomous or AI-powered systems can also make wrong decisions; adversaries can gain control and manipulate the AI's algorithm. That is why you must establish a robust cybersecurity measure to prevent malicious interference and ensure your autonomous systems continue to make the right decisions in high-stakes situations.

Complexity of AI Algorithms and Lack of Transparency: Lots of AI algorithms that are used in autonomous systems are mostly complex, and they operate as "black boxes," that is, it is not always straightforward to understand their decision-making processes, and even developers can have a hard time figuring it out. This shroud transparency contributes greatly to this poor understanding, making it more difficult to tell just how an AI-controlled autonomous system will respond exactly to a specific situation, especially when your system is infected with undesirable inputs. Also, it complicates efforts to secure these systems because you cannot possibly point out a potential vulnerability in an algorithm that tends to operate outside human comprehension. To build trust and ensure security in these autonomous systems, there is a need for advancements in explainable

AI(XAI); it makes decisions more interpretable.

Now, let's look into securing AI-based IoT ecosystems and smart infrastructure.

The IoT ecosystems constantly expand into cities, industries, and homes. Today, they have formed a backbone of what is now known as "smart infrastructure." From smart cities equipped with interconnected traffic systems to your industrial IoT (IIoT) that helps you monitor and optimize your factory operations, AI-powered IoT solutions bring greater control and efficiency. However, the extent of this interconnectedness also brings new security vulnerabilities that we need to address to protect our critical infrastructure and users. To secure our AI-based IoT and smart infrastructure, we must use:

End-to-end Encryption and Secure Data Transmission: End-to-end encryption is a fundamental security requirement for our IoT ecosystems. IoT devices are developed to generate and exchange massive amounts of sensitive data. If any form of interception happens to be on the way and this data is tempered, it can lead to a breach in security. End-to-end encryption secures transmitted data between the IoT devices and their controlling systems from unauthorized access. Suppose you're managing or deploying IoT devices. In that case, you need to implement secure data transmission protocols, such as Transport Layer Security (TLS) or IPsec, because they are essential tools for safeguarding transmitted data.

Authentication and Access Control Mechanisms: To prevent unauthorized access to your IoT devices and networks, you must implement a robust authentication and access control mechanism. With the diversities in IoT devices today, such as smart thermostats used in industrial sensors—it's vital to have a unique authentication process for each device. Biometric verification and multi-factor authentication (MFA) methods strengthen your security by limiting access to only verified devices and users. Implementing a Role-Based Access Control (RBAC) can also have great benefits because it can restrict device access according to the user's needs or roles, which helps minimize the risk of unauthorized manipulation.

AI-Driven Anomaly Detection: AI and its machine learning algorithms can enhance your

IoT security by continuously monitoring your device behavior to identify abnormal patterns that may indicate a cybersecurity threat. Let's say your IoT sensor embedded in your smart factory begins to transmit data at irregular or unusual values. The AI in the system can flag this strange behavior as suspicious, which calls for further investigation. Integrating anomaly detection into your AI-supported cybersecurity systems can create a more resilient IoT ecosystem against potential cybersecurity threats.

Device and Firmware Updates: IoT devices need regular firmware and software updates to protect against newly discovered vulnerabilities. However, managing these updates across many devices, especially in massive smart infrastructure deployments, comes with challenges. Automating updates of

AI-powered mechanisms can help you streamline this process and keep your devices secure without manual intervention. Having a mechanism that regularly updates your system is necessary if you're looking to maintain the integrity of the security of your IoT ecosystem while protecting it from emerging cyber threats.

Implementing Network Segmentation: Network segmentation involves dividing your organization's network into smaller, isolated segments. This approach can help your organization contain potential attacks that may spread by preventing them from going across the entire network. In your IoT ecosystems, segmenting critical devices from non-essential ones allows you to reduce the chances of a single breach compromising the entire system of your organization or IoT network. For instance, in smart city infrastructure, you can separate IoT devices handling traffic management from those used in environmental monitoring, which further strengthens your security by adding more layers of security to both systems.

User Awareness and Training: User awareness remains critical when thinking or discussing IoT security, even when robust cybersecurity measures are already in place. That's because when users and stakeholders are continually educated on the risks and best practices associated with their IoT, it improves general security by preventing incidents that could arise from human errors not educated about, such as improper device management or weak passwords. IoT's continuous adoption should spark a cybersecurity awareness culture because it is never important for individuals and organizations.

AI in Cyber Warfare and Nation-State Attacks

The risk of introducing AI into cyber warfare is best imagined, especially when nation-state actors leverage the advancements to fuel high-stakes cyberattacks, influence geopolitical conflicts, or target critical infrastructure. With sophisticated AI-driven tools, these adversaries can carry out efficient attacks and can evade detection faster. Nations must understand how these AI can precipitate future cyber warfare and devise defensive strategies to help mitigate these threats.

The Role of AI in cyber warfare goes beyond the predictable, traditional attack models. As we know, AI-powered tools can autonomously identify vulnerabilities, adapt their strategies based on real-time data, and even scale their operations to levels that have not been seen before. For instance, a generative AI system can create highly realistic, targeted phishing emails or synthetic media, such as deepfakes, to manipulate public perception, sow discord, and ferment trouble. According to the 2024 Homeland Threat Assessment by the Department of Homeland Security (DHS) of the USA, the proliferation of accessible AI tools has enhanced adversaries' tactics and has given them new means to undermine trust in government institutions, democratic processes, and social cohesion.

With the rapid pace at which AI cyber warfare is evolving, integrating AI into cybersecurity defenses has become more necessary than ever before. Even though the traditional cybersecurity measure still holds a degree of potency, it is still not adequate to deal with AI-enhanced threats of nation-states. So, whatever defensive cybersecurity tools we are looking at, they must possess the ability to adapt to sophisticated cyberattacks at the rate at which attackers' AI systems evolve, too.

The potential with which AI can transform cyber warfare is great, primarily due to its capacity to process a vast amount of data, automate decision-making processes, and identify patterns. Still, AI-powered tools can become an extremely potent tool in the hands of nation-state actors. AIso is capable of scanning infrastructural networks autonomously. They can scan critical infrastructure networks such as financial institutions, healthcare systems, and power grids to find weak spots that can be exploited with little or no human oversight. The precision and speed with which these attacks happen make AI a valuable tool for nation-states looking to deter or cause harm to a rival nation.

Today, generative AI can produce realistic text, images, and videos. It has become a powerful tool for threat actors who deploy them to produce convincing disinformation campaigns, create realistic synthetic media, and influence public opinion that blurs the line between reality and fiction. According to DHS, adversaries can craft persuasive lures tailored to each target, a development that can bring about distrust and destabilize our social systems. It creates direct threats and contributes to the larger destabilization of relations across borders.

AI-generated deepfakes can impersonate important individuals like political leaders or military personnel to incite panic, spread false information, or cause social unrest. Imagine a deepfake video showing a prominent leader making inciting statements capable of compromising national security. It can create confusion in the country, incite tensions, and even trigger economic repercussions before the truth comes to clear the air. AI can be weaponized to manipulate global narratives this way and can escalate conflicts on a geopolitical scale.

AI-powered devices can compromise sensitive data in cyberattacks, sabotage critical infrastructure, or steal proprietary technologies. Cyber espionage tactics can threaten our national security, as they can cause hostile entities to steal intellectual property or state secrets and gain strategic advantages on the global stage.

If nations and organizations must combat the evolving threats posed by AI-driven cyberattacks, they need to develop advanced cyber defense strategies and leverage AI capabilities. Integrating AI into defense systems would allow cybersecurity teams to comprehensively analyze data and automate responses to new threats and the rapid pace of cyber warfare.

By integrating AI into defense systems, cybersecurity professionals can analyze data more comprehensively, automate responses to emerging threats, and adapt to the rapid pace of cyber warfare. Here are some cyber defense strategies against AI-powered nation-state threats:

Continuous Monitoring and Real-Time Threat Detection: One of the key defensive strategies involves implementing AI-driven continuous monitoring systems. These systems use machine learning to analyze network traffic, identify abnormal behavior patterns, and detect potential threats in real time. By continuously analyzing data, AI-powered tools can detect unusual activities that may signify an impending attack, such as abnormal access attempts, uncharacteristic data movement, or changes in system performance, allowing for quicker identification of threats before they fully materialize.

AI's ability to identify anomalies at scale is particularly beneficial in large, complex networks, such as those found in critical infrastructure. These systems require constant vigilance to maintain security. Traditional methods, which rely on pre-defined threat signatures, may miss novel or evolving attacks. However, with AI-driven tools, AI can learn from past incidents and apply that knowledge to detect emerging threats, even those that deviate from known patterns.

Adaptive Defense Mechanisms: AI-powered defense systems can also respond and adapt to cyberattacks. AI systems can modify their responses based on the nature and scope of the threat. This flexibility is necessary when facing AI-driven attacks, which may change tactics and attempt to circumvent defenses. For example, AI systems can employ techniques like deception technology, which involves creating fake assets or honeypots that attract malicious actors. By diverting attackers from valuable resources, these systems can buy time for security teams to respond. Additionally, adaptive AI can help reroute network traffic, isolate compromised segments, or deploy patches dynamically while minimizing the impact of an attack.

Collaboration between Human Analysts and AI Systems: While AI can enhance cybersecurity defenses, human expertise remains invaluable. As the Department of Homeland Security posts, it's critical to integrate human oversight into AI-driven cybersecurity strategies. Cyber defense professionals bring contextual knowledge, experience, and ethical judgment, which AI systems lack. In cases where AI identifies potential threats, human analysts can investigate further, verify its findings, and make informed decisions about an appropriate response.

Collaboration between humans and AI is essential, especially when responding to sophisticated social engineering attacks, such as spear-phishing campaigns crafted using generative AI. Analyzing patterns in AI-generated communications allows human experts to identify tactics that AI systems might overlook. This hybrid human-AI collaboration approach gives faster, more accurate threat responses while ensuring all important ethical considerations are not left out during decision-making.

Investment in Quantum-Resistant and AI-Resistant Cryptography: The rise of quantum computing poses an additional challenge in cybersecurity. Quantum computers have the potential to break traditional encryption methods, which could expose sensitive data to malicious actors. Quantum-resistant cryptography is designed to withstand quantum attacks, especially on critical infrastructure and government agencies.

Also, AI-resistant cryptographic techniques are emerging as a defense against AI-powered cyber threats. Cryptographic algorithms that leverage AI in encryption can make it harder for adversaries to decrypt sensitive information. So, investing in these advanced cryptographic techniques can secure critical data and enhance AI capabilities.

Public Awareness and Cyber Hygiene: Besides advanced technical defenses, public awareness can play a vital role in cyber defense. Using generative AI for disinformation campaigns and social engineering attacks shows the importance of educating individuals about the risks. By promoting cybersecurity awareness, governments and organizations can encourage individuals to practice good cyber hygiene by verifying the authenticity of information, being cautious with email attachments, and recognizing phishing attempts.

Encouraging individuals to stay informed about emerging cyber threats strengthens overall cybersecurity resilience. Awareness campaigns can help individuals recognize potential disinformation, reducing the likelihood of widespread panic or misinformation-induced conflict. As AI-driven attacks become more prevalent, fostering a well-informed public can be one of the most effective defenses against nation-state cyber tactics.

CONCLUSION

AI and the Evolution of Cybersecurity

The advancements in AI and its applications in the field of cybersecurity have brought about fundamental changes in the outlook of cybersecurity today. However, these advancements come with their respective challenges. Therefore, organizations and security professionals must rethink their traditional models and adopt a more adaptable, forward-thinking approach.

AI's significant impact on cybersecurity is how it has transformed attack methodologies. AI has so far given cybercriminals the leverage to launch complex attacks with greater efficiency, cutting down on the time needed to plan and execute them. Traditional hacking techniques, such as phishing, malware distribution, and social engineering, are becoming more sophisticated with the introduction of AI algorithms, which help automate several hacking steps and personalize attacks, making them more difficult to detect. Such AI-driven methods of cyberattacks empower cybercriminals to craft deceptive messages that could mimic genuine communications to evade spam filters and target individuals or organizations with these messages with the intent to exploit their vulnerabilities. This dramatic shift puts cybersecurity teams on the edge, prompting them to anticipate increased attack frequency and sophistication, rendering traditional cybersecurity strategies insufficient.

AI-enhanced malware and ransomware attacks are increasing daily, compounding the existing cybersecurity problem. The AI's machine learning capabilities give malicious software the ability to adapt to security measures, bypass defenses, and even change their behavior when efforts are made to detect them. Today, malware are able to analyze an environment and fine-tune a suitable attack strategy, which effectively conceals its presence and maximizes the impact of the damage. For instance, AI-enabled ransomware can prioritize encrypting critical files and even backup systems before alerting users, thereby increasing the chances of a successful ransomware attack. Given the self-learning capabilities of malware they can manipulate their way to evade detection, mutate upon discovery, and reroute their code to bypass standard defenses which can create significant challenges for cybersecurity professionals.

The advent of AI has also spiked threat levels in identity fraud and unauthorized access. Techniques such as deepfakes, where AI are used to generate realistic synthetic media, give criminals the ability to impersonate executives or employees with unprecedented accuracy, often as part of targeted attacks aimed at bigger organizations. Deepfake technology has made it possible for threat actors to conduct impersonation attacks where voices and video feeds are manipulated to deceive employees and clients into giving up sensitive information or convince them to make unauthorized transfers. Such attacks have brought about new concerns when it comes to identity verification processes, causing organizations to seek advanced authentication systems to help them differentiate between real and fabricated identities.

Inspite of all these challenges discussed, AI remains a powerful cybersecurity defense tool. The AI machine learning algorithms are invaluable in identifying and analyzing anomalous patterns in an organization's network traffic, endpoint activity, and even user behavior, all of which can be indicator(s) of a potential cybersecurity threat. The capabilities of AI to process vast amounts of data in real-time give cybersecurity systems the ability to react instantaneously to potential threats, which can mitigate or prevent attacks altogether before they reach critical systems. For example, an AI-based intrusion detection system (IDS) and intrusion prevention system (IPS) functions by examining network traffic patterns, identify unusual behavior that could may be indicative of a possible breach, and then take preventive action. Additionally, AI-powered solutions are able to update

231

themselves continuosly based on new data which enables them to learn from each new threat landscape and adapt their response strategies accordingly.

The increasing adoption of AI in threat intelligence points towards a shift to more proactive cybersecurity practices. AI-based threat intelligence uses predictive analytics to identify trends and emerging threats, making it possible to anticipate and mitigate attacks, unlike traditional threat intelligence, which often relies on historical data. With data aggregation and advanced analytics, AI-enhanced threat intelligence tools can provide cybersecurity teams with more actionable insights, allowing them to address vulnerabilities and reduce attack surfaces preemptively. However, as AI continues to arm and improve the capabilities of both attackers and defenders, it has become increasingly necessary for organizations to maintain a dynamic approach to their cybersecurity that evolves as the face of these advancements.

Preparing for a Resilient Future

When talking about resilience in cybersecurity, it must be understood that it goes beyond simply preventing attacks; therefore, organizations must be able to adapt and recover quickly from security incidents while still maintaining their essential functions. As AI-driven threats become more sophisticated, cybersecurity systems must become equally resilient, and organizations must prioritize adaptable, multi-layered cybersecurity frameworks.

An essential element of cybersecurity resilience is continuous risk assessment, and AI can play a pivotal role in risk assessment and identification. This gives organizations the ability to address vulnerabilities before they are proactively exploited. Modern cybersecurity platforms rely on machine learning to allow them to continuously monitor unusual patterns in system activity, which provides a continuous risk assessment that highlights weak points within an organization's infrastructure. This ongoing process can help organizations stay ahead of attackers while directing resources toward strengthening defenses in areas most vulnerable to compromises.

Another important aspect when building cybersecurity resilience is the stress-testing of AI models used in cybersecurity systems. Subjecting AI-driven defense systems to simulated attacks allows organizations to identify and mitigate potential blind spots in their defenses. This kind of approach ensures that the AI algorithm remains effective in rapid and evolving cyber threats. It does it by forcing systems to adapt to new attack vectors and refine their response mechanisms accordingly. Regular testing can also help organizations refine their incident response strategies, making it possible to respond to actual security incidents with greater speed and confidence.

Automation and adaptive learning are essential in building resilience in a cybersecurity environment that is enhanced by AI. With automated defenses, organizations can respond to threats faster, due to the reduced time between detection and response that happens in seconds or milliseconds. AI-driven automation is invaluable when addressing common attack patterns, as it gives security systems the leverage to neutralize lower-level threats without the need for human intervention. AI's adaptive learning capabilities can equally allow cybersecurity systems to adjust their approach to new threats by learning from each security incident, which helps them evolve their detection methods.

Employee training is also another vital component of building cybersecurity resilience. As more sophisticated AI-driven cyberattacks grow, so do the targets in human vulnerabilities. That is why every employee within an organization must understand these threats and recognize signs of phishing, social engineering, and other forms of cyber manipulation. So, training programs should be encouraged and focused on raising awareness of these AI-enhanced threats and teaching employees how to respond to suspicious activities. Doing so would ultimately transform the workforce into an additional layer of defense.

Another important element of resilience in an AI-driven threat landscape is proactive intelligence, and by leveraging AI for predictive analysis, organizations can gain insight into emerging trends and potential attack vectors. This allows them to allocate resources and implement countermeasures before threats materialize. With proactive intelligence, organizations would have an early warning system that empowers them to strengthen defenses, monitor potential adversaries, and mitigate risks, creating a more resilient security posture capable of withstanding future threats.

Capabilities of Modern SIEM Tools in the AI Context

The evolution of security information and event management (SIEM) tools has made them vital components of an AI-driven cybersecurity strategy. Modern SIEM tools powered by AI and machine learning give organizations the capabilities of advanced threat detection to identify and respond to security incidents with greater speed and accuracy. This kind of transformation has impactfully positioned SIEM in cybersecurity; helping organizations to achieve comprehensive situational awareness and a proactive security posture.

AI-enhanced SIEM platforms can take and analyze vast amounts of data from diverse sources, including network traffic, endpoint activity, and even application logs. Machine learning algorithms then sift through this data, identifying correlations and patterns that may indicate security threats. This capability allows SIEM tools to detect anomalous behavior, like unusual login attempts, unauthorized data access, or a sudden spikes in network traffic. AI-driven SIEM tools can identify unknown threats by focusing on patterns rather than specific attack signatures, making it possible to detect novel attacks that may evade traditional security measures.

An important benefit of AI in SIEM is the reduction of false positives, which is often a common issue in traditional SIEM systems. As machine learning is able to distinguish between normal variations in activity and potential security threats, AI-enhanced SIEM platforms can significantly reduce the number of false alerts that security teams must address. Such an improvement enables cybersecurity professionals to focus on genuine threats, increasing efficiency and improving response time. Therefore, AI-driven SIEM tools enhance threat detection and optimize resource allocation within security teams.

Incident response is yet another area where AI has enhanced the SIEM tool's capabilities.

Modern SIEM platforms use AI to automate incident response workflows and allow security systems to take prompt action when a threat is detected. For instance, let's say an AI-driven SIEM platform identifies a suspicious login attempt: after detecting such activity, it can automatically block the user, notify security personnel, and trigger additional security measures to contain the threat. This level of automation gives organizations the capability to address time-sensitive threats, minimizing the delay between detection and response, thereby reducing the potential damage caused by a security incident.

Integrating AI with SIEM has also enhanced situational awareness within cybersecurity operations. While data are aggregated from multiple sources and correlated in real-time, AI-driven SIEM platforms provide security teams with a comprehensive view of the organization's security posture. This kind of centralized approach enables teams to look out for threats across all areas of the network to have greater visibility and control over potential vulnerabilities. So, enhanced situational awareness is especially important in today's complex threat environment because it allows security teams to detect and respond to sophisticated, multi-stage attacks that might otherwise go unnoticed in traditional, siloed security models.

Lastly, AI-enabled SIEM tools are capable of supporting continuous improvement within cybersecurity operations. , these tools refine their detection and response capabilities over time to analyze the effectiveness of each response and learn from previous incidents, creating a feedback loop that enhances the organization's overall resilience. Such a continuous learning process allows security teams to stay ahead of emerging threats while ensuring that the SIEM system remains updated with the latest threat intelligence and defensive strategies.

The Transformative Potential of AI in Cybersecurity

Integration of AI into cybersecurity has brought about a fundamental transformation in how organizations approach their digital defenses. The capabilities of AIs to analyze vast data sets, identify complex patterns, and adapt to new threats have opened up new possibilities for securing digital environments. Still, the same capabilities that have made AI a powerful defense tool can also be employed by malicious actors, bringing about a dynamic and evolving threat landscape.

Achieving a Balance: Opportunity and Responsibility

There is a delicate balance between opportunities and responsibilities that characterizes AI's impact on cybersecurity. On one hand, AI can offer an unprecedented opportunity to enhance security, streamline incident response, and improve situational awareness. On the other hand, there is potential misuse, which raises ethical and applicability concerns, particularly as attackers continue to exploit these capabilities for malicious purposes. With the continued evolution of AI, cybersecurity professionals, policymakers, and organizations must work together to establish ethical guidelines, regulatory frameworks, and best practices that help govern the use of AI in cybersecurity.

Adapting to the Future: Continuous Learning and Collaboration

The future of cybersecurity in an AI-driven world depends on a commitment to continuous learning and collaboration across various industries. Cybersecurity teams must remain vigilant and adapt their strategies and defenses as new AI-driven threats emerge. So, collaborating with AI developers, researchers, and industry peers will be essential in sharing knowledge, identifying emerging threats, and developing innovative solutions one step ahead of cybercriminals and their tactics.

A Call to Action for Organizations and Security Professionals

As we move into an era of increasingly sophisticated cyber threats, organizations must take proactive steps to protect their digital assets, data, and users. To do this, organizations must commit to investing in AI-enhanced cybersecurity solutions, fostering a culture of cybersecurity awareness while refining their security practices constantly to address the unique challenges posed by AI-driven threats. Embracing a forward-thinking approach allows organizations to build a resilient cybersecurity posture that would be ready to face the evolving challenges of this digital age.

GLOSSARY OF KEY TERMS

Advanced Encryption Standard (AES): it is an encryption standard that is widely used for data protection. AES can encrypt sensitive information to prevent unauthorized access, which are crucial in AI-driven security measures to secure data and prevent breaches in cybersecurity.

Advanced Persistent Threats (APTs): The APTs are prolonged cyberattacks that are often targeted at specific data and rely on the use sophisticated techniques to infiltrate systems undetected. AI-powered cybersecurity tools can detect APT patterns which enhance threat identification and response.

Adversarial Machine Learning: this is a field AI that is concerned with the understanding of how machine learning models can be deceived or manipulated by malicious input. It is important in cybersecurity in identifying and mitigating attacks that attempt to bypass AI systems.

Adversarial Training: it is a method used to train machine learning models to improve robustness. The chances of AI of AI models being compromised by adversarial attacks can be reduced with adversarial training, strengthening cybersecurity measures.

AI Datasets: They are datasets that are used to train and test AI models. Curated AI datasets can help in building more effective models for anomaly detection, intrusion detection, and predictive analytics during security operations in cybersecurity.

AI Models: They are algorithms and neural networks that are used to process and analyze data. AI models can detect threats, predict potential vulnerabilities, and automate security tasks in cybersecurity

AI-based SIEM: This is an evolution of traditional Security Information and Event Management (SIEM) systems that leverages AI to analyze large data volumes in real-time. These systems can improve threat detection accuracy and reduce incident response times.

AI-driven Cybersecurity Tools: They are tools that rely on AI to enhance cybersecurity measures, such as threat detection, behavioral analysis, and automated response. These tools are critical when it comes to defending against modern, sophisticated cyber threats.

Algorithm Bias: An algorithm bias is phenomenon where AI models exhibit biased behavior as a result of skewed training data. Addressing algorithm bias is necessary for ensuring fair and accurate threat detection across diverse datasets in cybersecurity.

Anomaly Detection: it involves identifying patterns that may deviate from expected behavior. AI-based anomaly detection is an essential component in cybersecurity, used to spot suspicious activities that may be indicative of a cybersecurity threat.

Antivirus: These are Software, designed to detect and prevent malware. Modern antivirus programs use AI for advanced threat detection, thereby enhancing cybersecurity resilience against viruses and malware.

API Call Spikes: They are a sudden increases in API requests that often indicates potential cyberattacks. Monitoring API call spikes with AI allows for early detection of threats like DDoS attacks.

Artificial Intelligence (AI): This is a simulation of human intelligence by machines with applications in cybersecurity for threat detection, automation, and enhanced security analytics.

Automation: it is the use of technology to perform tasks without human intervention. AI-enabled automation is pivotal when dealing with routine security tasks, as it allows for faster incident response.

AWS CloudTrail Logs: They are Logs provided by Amazon Web Services to monitor user activity and API usage. AI systems can analyze these logs to detect unusual patterns that may indicate a security breach.

Backdoor Poisoning: it is a form of cyberattack in which attackers inserts malicious data into AI training datasets to create a "backdoor." This type of attack points to the need for robust AI and data validation in cybersecurity.

Behavioral Analytics: With this, systems can analyze user behavior and use that knowledge in detecting abnormal patterns. AI-powered behavioral analytics can identify potential security risks based on deviations from the normal behavior in cybersecurity.

Black-box attacks: they are attacks in which adversaries attempt to exploit a system even when they know nothing about its internal workings. AI-based systems are designed to defend against such attacks by continuously adapting to unknown threat patterns.

Brute Forcing: it is a method used to gain unauthorized access by guessing all manners of passwords. AI systems in cybersecurity can help detect and block brute-force attempts by monitoring login patterns and unusual access attempts.

California Consumer Privacy Act (CCPA): it is a privacy law that protects the rights of California residents over their data. Compliance with CCPA is vital in AI-driven cybersecurity practices to protect user privacy and avoiding consequences of a default.

ChatGPT: it is an AI language model that is capable of generating text. Its relevance in cybersecurity can be seen in automated responses and potential vulnerabilities related to misuse of language models in social engineering.

Corporate Espionage: this is an intellectual property theft of sensitive data to gain competitive advantage over rivals. AI systems in cybersecurity are capable of preventing corporate espionage by securing data and identifying unusual access behaviors.

Cyber Threats: these are malicious activities that are aimed at disrupting, damaging, or gaining unauthorized access to information systems. AI can enhance cybersecurity by predicting, detecting, and mitigating such threats in real time.

Cyberattacks: They are deliberate exploits on computer systems and networks to steal, alter, or destroy data. AI-driven tools can be employed to accurately identify, analyze, and prevent these attacks.

Cybersecurity: it is a deliberate effort employed in protecting systems, networks, and data from cyberattacks. Integrating AI technologies in cybersecurity improved detection, response, and resilience against emerging threats.

Data: This information can be analyzed and processed. AI uses data to detect trends, recognize anomalies, and predict potential vulnerabilities in cybersecurity.

Deep Neural Networks (DNN): These are a class of machine learning algorithms that can mimic the human brain structure. DNNs can play a role in cybersecurity by identifying complex patterns in data which are useful in detecting sophisticated threats.

Defensive Distillation: this is a method for enhancing AI model robustness against adversarial attacks. Defensive distillation can help to create resilient AI systems that are less vulnerable to adversarial manipulation in cybersecurity.

Differential Privacy: this is a technique that ensures privacy in data analysis. Differential privacy is used to protect sensitive information while allowing AI-driven analysis in cybersecurity.

DNS Logs are records of Domain Name System queries. AI can analyze DNS logs to detect potential threats, such as malware that relies on DNS for command-and-control communication.

Elliptic Curve Cryptography (ECC) is a type of encryption that is based on elliptic curves, which provides stronger security. ECC can be used in cybersecurity to secure communications without sacrificing speed.

Endpoints: these are devices that serve as network entry points. AI-powered cybersecurity solutions can monitor and secure endpoints so as to prevent unauthorized access and protect against malware.

Explainable AI: they are AI models. Designed to be transparent in its decision-making. In cybersecurity, explainable AI is crucial in helping organizations gain trust in

AI-driven threat detection and response systems.

False Positives: they are incorrect alerts generated by a security system. AI can improve cybersecurity by reducing false positives, and allow analysts to focus on actual threats.

GenAI: Generative AI technology can be used to create content. They can support threat levels of intelligence and equally pose risks if used to generate malicious content.

Generative Adversarial Networks (GANs): These are AI models used to generate realistic data. GANs are often have dual-use in cybersecurity; they can enhance simulations for training or potentially generate deceptive data.

GPT: it is a transformer-based AI model that is known for natural language processing. GPT models can help automate responses and improve threat intelligence, but they require cautious use to prevent misuse.

Gradient-Based Attacks: These are techniques employed by malicious attackers to exploit AI models by adjusting inputs to cause model misclassification. It cybersecurity priority to protect AI systems and defend against such attacks

Grover's Algorithm: This is a quantum computing algorithm that is used to search for faster data. Quantum computing advancements come with significant implications for cybersecurity, especially for breaking cryptographic systems.

Identity Verification: It is the process of confirming user identity. AI-powered identity verification is critical in cybersecurity for a more secure authentication and access control.

Intellectual Property (IP): These are creative or proprietary information valuable to an organization. Protecting an IP with AI-driven cybersecurity can prevent data theft and corporate espionage.

Intrusion Detection Systems (IDS): These are systems designed to monitor network traffic for suspicious activity. AI-enhanced IDS can improve detection accuracy and adapt to new threats.

IoT Devices: They are internet-connected devices that can be vulnerable to cyber threats. AI solutions can help secure IoT networks by identifying abnormal patterns and preventing intrusions.

IPsec: This is a protocol suite that can be used to secure Internet communication. AI-based cybersecurity ensures robust IPsec implementation which adds a layer of security for remote communication.

Label Poisoning: This is a type of attack where labels in training data are altered to mislead AI models. Protecting datasets against label poisoning is vital in AI-based cybersecurity.

Machine Learning: This is a subset of AI that is focused on pattern recognition and prediction. Machine learning is foundational to cybersecurity for threat detection, anomaly identification, and automation.

Model Evasion Attacks: They are a form of attacks where adversaries bypass an AI model's defenses. AI-based cybersecurity systems must be designed in a way to detect and mitigate evasion tactics.

Model Inversion Attacks: This is a privacy attack that aims to reconstruct input data from an AI model. Defending against model inversion is critical to protect sensitive information in cybersecurity.

Multi-Factor Authentication (MFA): They are an authentication process that requires multiple verification steps. AI can support MFA by adapting security measures based on user behavior.

Natural Language Processing (NLP): This is a branch of AI that deals with human language understanding. NLP assists in analyzing communication for signs of phishing or social engineering.

Netflix: Netflix is a streaming platform that applies AI to understand user preferences. Similar AI techniques are used to identify user behavior patterns, which help detect unauthorized activities and anomalies in cybersecurity.

Network Security: it is a way of protecting network infrastructure from threats and breaches. AI-driven network security can provide real-time monitoring, threat detection, and automated responses to defend against advanced cyber threats.

PassGAN AI: This is an AI model that can generate realistic passwords for password security analysis. Tools like PassGAN help to assess password strength which shows the need for strong password policies to counter AI-aided brute-forcing.

Personally Identifiable Information (PII): They are sensitive information that can identify individuals, like their names or Social Security numbers. AI-driven cybersecurity solutions ensures the protection of PII by detecting and mitigating risks that are associated with data exposure.

Poisoning Attacks: These are yet another form of attacks that corrupt the training data of AI models, degrading their performance. Poisoning attacks can compromise AI's effectiveness, making it critical to validate and monitor data quality in cybersecurity systems.

Predictive Analytics: It is the Use of data, statistical algorithms, and machine learning to identify the likelihood of future outcomes. Predictive analytics can anticipate potential threats, allowing proactive measures to be taken in cybersecurity.

Privacy: This is the protection of individuals' data. AI in cybersecurity allows for enforcement of privacy regulations and policies thereby safeguarding sensitive data from unauthorized access.

Quantum AI: They are AI applied to quantum computing which enhances processing power for complex problems. Quantum AI can revolutionize encryption and threat detection, posing new risks with quantum-enabled attacks in cybersecurity.

Quantum Computing: It is a computing technology that leverages quantum mechanics to process information.

Quantum computing can have a great impact on cybersecurity by potentially breaking current encryption standards, making AI-aided quantum-resistant encryption essential.

Quantum-Based Threats: They are cyber threats that are enabled by quantum computing and can potentially break traditional encryption algorithms. To protect against quantum-enabled attacks, advancements in AI-driven cybersecurity defenses are necessary.

Ransomware: They are malicious software that encrypts files and demands ransom for their release. AI aids in identifying ransomware signatures and mitigating attacks before they lock critical systems.

Reverse-Engineering: It is a way of analyzing software or systems to understand their functionality or replicate them. With reverse engineering security teams can identify vulnerabilities in AI models to prevent their exploitation by malicious actors in cybersecurity.

Rivest-Shamir-Adleman (RSA): It is a widely used encryption algorithm that secures digital data. RSA faces challenges with advancing AI and quantum technologies and requires updates to maintain robust encryption in cybersecurity.

Robustness: It is the ability of a system to handle various challenges without failure. A robust AI model can withstand adversarial attacks and maintain reliability in threat detection.

Sentiment Analysis: It is an AI-powered analysis that is used to interpret emotions in text. In cybersecurity, sentiment analysis can help detect phishing attempts or insider threats by analyzing unusual language patterns.

Signature-Based Detection: This is a method of identifying threats using known malware signatures. AI enhances signature-based detection by identifying evolving threats that traditional signatures may not capture.

Social Engineering: It is a manipulation technique that exploits human psychology to gain unauthorized access to systems or data. AI aids in detecting social engineering by identifying abnormal communication patterns and potential phishing attempts in cybersecurity.

Spoofing: These are a form of attack where a malicious entity disguises itself as a trusted source. AI-driven cybersecurity systems analyze traffic patterns and detect spoofing attempts in emails, IP addresses, and websites to prevent unauthorized access.

Supply Chain Attack: It is an attack that targets vulnerabilities within an organization's supply chain, impacting partners and suppliers. AI enhances supply chain security by monitoring and identifying potential risks from third-party software or vendors.

Threat Actor: They are individuals or a group of people with malicious intent to compromise security. AI in cybersecurity categorizes and tracks threat actor behaviors, enabling proactive defenses and adaptive threat intelligence.

Threat Intelligence: They are information that helps organizations understand, identify, and respond to cyber threats. AI-powered threat intelligence analyzes massive amounts of data, providing insights into emerging threats and enhancing cybersecurity posture.

Tokenization: This is a process of replacing sensitive data with unique identifiers or tokens. AI helps manage tokenization by ensuring that sensitive data is protected across applications and networks, reducing the risk of exposure.

Two-Factor Authentication (2FA): it is a security process that requires two verification forms for access. In cybersecurity, AI strengthens 2FA by detecting anomalies in access behavior and enhancing overall authentication processes.

User and Entity Behavior Analytics (UEBA): They are AI-powered technology that monitors user and entity activities to detect abnormal behaviors that may indicate security risks. UEBA is crucial for identifying insider threats and unusual activities within networks.

Virtual Private Network (VPN): This is a tool that encrypts internet traffic, providing secure remote access to networks. In AI-driven cybersecurity, VPN usage is monitored for potential threats or abnormal behavior that could signify compromised connections.

Vishing: It is a form of phishing conducted via phone calls or voice messages. AI-driven voice analytics helps detect and block vishing attempts by identifying suspicious language patterns and abnormal call activity.

Vulnerability: They are weaknesses in a system that attackers can exploit. AI in cybersecurity continuously scans for vulnerabilities and provides risk assessments, enabling organizations to prioritize and address security gaps.

Watering Hole Attack: They are targeted attacks where a malicious actor infects websites commonly visited by a specific group to compromise their devices. AI-driven threat intelligence can help identify compromised sites and protect users against these attacks.

Whaling Attack: it is a phishing attack targeted at high-level executives or "big fish" within an organization. AI improves phishing detection by analyzing language and behavior, enabling more robust protection against such targeted attacks.

White-Hat Hacker: this is an ethical hacker who uses hacking skills to identify and fix security vulnerabilities. In cybersecurity, white-hat hackers leverage AI tools for vulnerability testing, strengthening systems against potential attacks.

Zero-Day Exploit: This is a cyberattack that targets a previously unknown vulnerability. AI enhances the detection and response to zero-day exploits by identifying unusual patterns and behaviors that signify emerging threats.

Zero Trust Architecture: it is a security model that requires strict verification for every user and device attempting access. AI in cybersecurity strengthens zero trust by continuously assessing access requests reducing risks associated with unauthorized access.

REFERENCES

Accenture. (2023). *AI in Business: Accelerating Adoption with Caution.* Retrieved from https://www.accenture.com

Accenture. (2023). *Addressing Algorithmic Bias in Cybersecurity AI Models.* Retrieved from https://www.accenture.com

Accenture. (2023). *The Impact of AI Accuracy on Cybersecurity.* Retrieved from https://www.accenture.com

Brand Times. (2023). *Just 11% of CIOs have fully implemented AI as data and security concerns hinder adoption.* Retrieved from https://www.brandtimes.com.ng

Deloitte. (2023). *The Role of AI in Business Success: CIO Perspectives.* Retrieved from https://www2.deloitte.com

European Data Protection Board. (2022). *AI and GDPR Compliance Report.* Retrieved from https://edpb.europa.eu

Gartner. (2023). *Impact of User Bias in Cybersecurity AI Predictions.* Retrieved from https://www.gartner.com

IBM. (2024). *Cost of a Data Breach Report.* Retrieved from https://www.ibm.com

MDPI. (2021). *Adversarial Attacks and Defense Mechanisms in Machine Learning.* Retrieved from https://www.mdpi.com/2413-4155/6/1/3

MIT. (2022). *Study on Bias in AI Applications.* Retrieved from https://www.mit.edu

Palo Alto Networks. (n.d.). *What are adversarial attacks on AI Machine Learning?.* Retrieved from https://www.paloaltonetworks.com

Ponemon Institute. (2022). *State of AI and Data Bias in Cybersecurity.* Retrieved from https://www.ponemon.org

Ponemon Institute. (2022). *State of Alert Fatigue in Cybersecurity.* Retrieved from https://www.ponemon.org

Bloomberg. (2024, June 26). *Evolve Bank &*
Trust confirms its data was stolen in cyber attack.
Retrieved from
https://www.bloomberg.com/news/articles/
2024-06-26/evolve-bank-trust-confirms-its-
data-was-stolen-in-cyber-attack

FCA. (2024). *FCA fines Tesco Bank for failures in*
2016 cyber attack. Retrieved from
https://www.fca.org.uk/news/press-
releases/fca-fines-tesco-bank-failures-2016-
cyber-attack

Pharmaceutical Technology. (2024). *Pharma*
cyber attacks: The growing threat to healthcare data.
Retrieved from https://www.pharmaceutical-
technology.com/features/pharma-cyber-
attacks/

Sophos. (2024). *AI in Cybersecurity: Enhancing*
protection through advanced technology. Retrieved

from https://www.sophos.com/en-us/cybersecurity-explained/ai-in-cybersecurity

The Guardian. (2024, May 17). *UK engineering giant Arup falls victim to deepfake scam targeting Hong Kong project.* Retrieved from https://www.theguardian.com/technology/article/2024/may/17/uk-engineering-arup-deepfake-scam-hong-kong-ai-video

IT Governance. (2024). *AI scams: Real-life examples and how to defend against them.* Retrieved from https://www.itgovernance.eu/blog/en/ai-scams-real-life-examples-and-how-to-defend-against-them

Integrity.pt. (2024). *Voice deepfake threats and real-life cases.* Retrieved from https://www.integrity.pt/real-life/voice-deepfake.html

CNN. (2024, February 4). *Deepfake CFO scam rocks Hong Kong corporate landscape.* Retrieved from

https://edition.cnn.com/2024/02/04/asia/deepfake-cfo-scam-hong-kong-intl-hnk/index.html

New Scientist. (2024). *The deepfakes of Trump and Biden that you are most likely to fall for.* Retrieved from

https://www.newscientist.com/article/2447853-the-deepfakes-of-trump-and-biden-that-you-are-most-likely-to-fall-for/

NPR. (2024, May 23). *FCC tackles AI deepfake robocall scandal involving Biden impersonation.* Retrieved from

https://www.npr.org/2024/05/23/nx-s1-4977582/fcc-ai-deepfake-robocall-biden-new-hampshire-political-operative

Forbes. (2024, April 15). *The future of cybersecurity is zero trust & AI.* Retrieved from https://www.forbes.com/sites/zscaler/2024/04/15/the-future-of-cybersecurity-is-zero-trust--ai/

Springer Open. (2024). *Understanding zero-trust AI through enhanced threat analysis.* Retrieved from https://jesit.springeropen.com/articles/10.1186/s43067-024-00155-z

Checkpoint. (2024). *Zero Trust AI Access: New era in cybersecurity.* Retrieved from https://www.checkpoint.com/cyber-hub/cyber-security/what-is-ai-security/what-is-zero-trust-ai-access-ztai/

Silobreaker. (2024). *AI in Threat Intelligence.* Retrieved from https://www.silobreaker.com/glossary/ai-in-threat-intelligence/

Microsoft Tech Community. (2024). *How AI can improve threat intelligence gathering and usage.* Retrieved from https://techcommunity.microsoft.com/t5/educator-developer-blog/how-ai-can-improve-threat-intelligence-gathering-and-usage/ba-p/3975449

Simplilearn. (2024). *Challenges of Artificial Intelligence: Potential and Limitations.* Retrieved from https://www.simplilearn.com/challenges-of-artificial-intelligence-article

SCIRP. (2024). *AI challenges and advancements in business applications.* Retrieved from https://www.scirp.org/journal/paperinformation?paperid=134347

Clanx.ai. (2024). *Human-AI Collaboration: Benefits and obstacles.* Retrieved from https://clanx.ai/glossary/human-ai-colaboration

Journal of the Academy of Management Review. (2024). *Examining human-AI collaboration dynamics.* Retrieved from https://journals.aom.org/doi/10.5465/amr.2021.0421

Xponent21. (2024). *Managing AI limitations: Balancing automation with human oversight.* Retrieved from https://xponent21.com/insights/managing-ai-limitations-the-essential-balance-of-automation-and-human-oversight/

ResearchGate. (2024). *Quantum Computing and AI: Implications for cybersecurity.* Retrieved from https://www.researchgate.net/publication/375000512_Quantum_Computing_and_AI_Implications_for_Cybersecurity

NextGov. (2023, September). *DOE unveils $39 million in electric grid cybersecurity projects.* Retrieved from https://www.nextgov.com/cybersecurity/2023/09/doe-unveils-39-million-electric-grid-cybersecurity-projects/390226/

NextGov. (2023, September). *New Pentagon cyber strategy emphasizes industry and global partnerships.* Retrieved from https://www.nextgov.com/cybersecurity/2023/09/new-pentagon-cyber-strategy-emphasizes-industry-and-global-partnerships/390265/

The Hacker News. (2024, February). *Microsoft, OpenAI warn of nation-state cyber threats exploiting AI.* Retrieved from https://thehackernews.com/2024/02/microsoft-openai-warn-of-nation-state.html

INDEX

285